The

Pink Palace

Behind Closed Doors at the
Beverly Hills Hotel

Sandra Lee Stuart

LYLE STUART Inc. • Secaucus, New Jersey

First edition   Design by Janet Anderson
Copyright ® 1978 by Sandra Lee Stuart
All rights reserved, including the right to reproduce
this book or any portion thereof in any form.
Published by Lyle Stuart Inc.
120 Enterprise Ave., Secaucus, N.J. 07094

Published simultaneously in Canada by George J. McLeod Limited
Don Mills, Ontario

Address queries regarding rights and permissions to Lyle Stuart

Manufactured in the United States of America

Library of Congress Cataloging in Publication Data

Stuart, Sandra Lee.
   The pink palace.

   Includes index.
   1. Beverly Hills Hotel. I. Title.
TX941.B48S78   647'.94794'94   78-12519
ISBN 0-8184-0246-6

To the men I love most.

To Mark.   To Rory.

To Dad.

ACKNOWLEDGMENTS

If there had been no John, there would have been no book.
If there had been no Mona, there would have been no book.
If there had been no Mark, there would have been no book.
No Lyle, no Carole, no Barbara, no book.

Thanks to you all.

S L S

July 12, 1978

Part One

Chapter One

Kings

It wasn't as if Clark Gable could take Carole Lombard just anywhere.

A seedy hotel stained with reminders of other trysts was hardly the proper setting for a rendezvous between Hollywood's highest-paid actress and its crowned head. On the other hand, most of the first-class hotels were too visible for a couple of highly visible stars, one of them still married, whose studios would frown on flagrant hankypanky. Affairs were fine, but they must be kept behind closed doors and out of print.

Still, the solution was easy. Gable had a third party register under a false name and secure a key to one of the bungalows nestled deep in palms and jacarandas. A duplicate was made and passed on to Lombard. At the appointed time, Gable and Lombard arrived by separate garden paths, circumventing the lobby, scurrying to their castle away from home, their Pink Palace.

Queens

Queen Juliana of the Netherlands was due to arrive on a state visit. To honor her, the keepers of the castle planted three beds of violet and gold tulips around her bungalow, bungalow 5.

Lo and behold—and as such things should happen—the tulips bloomed within hours of the queen's arrival.

Not surprising at the Pink Palace.

Princes

It threw the keepers of the castle at first, but royalty is royalty, and if Prince Philip, consort to Elizabeth, wanted to pick all the fruit from the orange tree outside his door, so be it.

Princesses

Svend, the Olympian guardian of the pool, has seen them all, from Monroe to Welch, but the one he had goose-bumps for was Grace Kelly. She had checked in, and Svend had been told she was heading for the pool.

All day he waited. Royalty, of both Hollywood and hereditary varieties, didn't awe Svend ordinarily—he treated everyone with the same good humor and solic- itude. But Grace—well, she was something special, beauty incarnate and all that.

Finally Svend moaned that Grace was an apparent no-show.

"Didn't you see her?" someone asked him. She had been there all afternoon, that pleasant, tiny-bit-plump matron playing with her kids at poolside.

Jacks

The 1960 presidential campaign was in full and grueling swing. The senator from Massachusetts was officially reg- istered at the Beverly Hilton while he was stumping in Los Angeles. Unofficially and very hush-hush, John Fitzgerald kept a Jackie-less bungalow at the Pink Palace for entertaining the likes of Judith Campbell Exner, Angie Dickinson, Marilyn Monroe, and sundry starlets who caught his fancy.

Jokers

W. C. Fields walked into the Polo Lounge, the Pink Palace's famed tippling room, and asked for a table for two—a seat for him and another for his man-eating plant.

They were seated, no eyebrows raised.

§   §   §   §   §   §   §   §   §   §

The Pink Palace, otherwise known as the Beverly Hills Hotel.

For sixty-six years the meeting place, trysting spot, love nest, cloister, front stage, home, and waystop for the beautiful, the rich, the powerful—for people made familiar to us by newspaper headlines and television close-ups. Men and women born to luxury and those who scrambled for it. And for others who are neither notorious nor famous but pass the credit check and don't mind paying for luxury and the titillation of being in the same bungalow where Gable bedded Lombard or the one once occupied by Juliana, or of sitting next to Charlie's Angels in the Polo Lounge.

They've all come to the Beverly Hills Hotel. Behind its closed doors affairs and marriages have started and ended. Multimillion-dollar businesses bought and sold. There have been births and deaths. Episodes sordid and silly, and many of them worth telling.

There's a specialness about the Beverly Hills, in its stubborn refusal to give in to the corporate and conglomerate monotony that has overcome most of the hotels in America today. The new ones are being built to look alike and to cater to conventions and package-tour guests. There, breakfast is instant coffee and mass-toasted white bread. The old ones are losing their character and charm to business-school mentalities whose only consideration is the ledger sheet.

As Ada Louise Huxtable of the *New York Times* has noted,

> Today's hotels are designed by convention specialists and computers and furnished from the sales and supply rooms of something euphemistically called the hospitality industry. ... Most new hotels are like airports; they follow a standardized formula that makes all cities look alike. The same plans, rooms, and fixtures depersonalize both people and places....
>
> Ice and Coke machines stand in the halls; cold toast in aluminum foil on plastic trays have replaced the rose on the room service table. If the rose comes, it is wilted.

The roses are still perfect at the Beverly Hills Hotel.

It hasn't followed many of the old hotels, bowing to convenience foods or the wrecking ball. Anachronistic in its insistence on service—the little touches and the bigger ones—the Beverly Hills is one of the most successful hotels in the world. It can afford to stick to its old ways, because it has that extra card up its sleeve. It's got Hollywood, or what's left of it. It's got the cast and the scenery for all those *nouveau riche* who want to further their American Dream by rubbing shoulders with the stars and breathing in the atmosphere of what went on and who was there years ago in what *The Rich and the Super-Rich* author Ferdinand Lundberg calls the "Shangri-la for newcomers."

For they all come to the Beverly Hills Hotel, if not to stay, then to mix and mingle in the Polo Lounge. One English journalist was lamenting, not long ago, that Hollywood–Beverly Hills was a dud, a disappointment. Not once did he stand behind Barbra Streisand on a supermarket line, nor did he purchase Band-Aids next to Charlton Heston in Thrifty Drugs. It was a washout. After weeks of peering into the windows of Rolls-Royces, he had seen only a lot of unfamiliar suntanned faces under piles of overstyled hair.

But then one day he happened into the Beverly Hills Hotel, where he saw someone who looked "incredibly" like Michael Caine sitting at the bar. A few minutes later while waiting for a phone in the lobby, "it occurred to me that the man already occupying the booth was Warren Beatty, and I was about to remark this to the character in front of me, when I realized the character in front of me was Ringo Starr. I was suddenly overwhelmed by the fact that this place wasn't myth, but actually real!"

The "myth" of the place is the place. The glamour attracts power. The glamour attracts sycophants. The glamour attracts the up-and-coming-yearning-to-breathe-the-rarefied-air. The glamour attracts more glamour. No matter how cynical or aloof to the phenomenon, few are immune. It kind of hits you like a bad case of flu. The best remedy is to order an orange blossom in the Polo Lounge or check into bungalow 4.

President Sukarno of Indonesia was in the Polo Lounge drinking something (unrecorded for history), when a vision of voluptuousness and sexuality sashayed across his range of vision.

"Who," he demanded, *"is* that blonde woman?"

When told it was Marilyn Monroe, Sukarno upped and moved a good part of his entourage of two hundred (including his official food taster) from the Ambassador to the Beverly Hills. It was enough just to share airspace with Monroe, even for the ruler of 130 million people.

There is always the hope that the fantasy of the place will come true, will reach out and suck you in. Once, Monroe, object of so many dreams, got into a conversation with a fellow guest one night while passing time in the Polo Lounge. They found they had something in common—both were temporarily mateless. Monroe's husband at the time, Arthur Miller, had left on business.

The fellow's wife had yet to arrive. Nice conversation; it ended soon.

The fellow returned to his bungalow and got ready for bed. Knock at the door. It was Marilyn. She wanted to model the outfit underneath her fur coat. What did the fellow think of it? she asked, throwing open her coat. The fellow thought an awful lot of it. So had most other American males. The outfit was Marilyn.

"What could I do?" the fellow later asked a friend. "I'm a man, after all. I invited her in."

The hijinks and the history of the place are all there, drifting enticingly by, mixing with the scents of gardenia and ginger.

This is where H. R. Haldeman and friends got word that their Watergate burglars had botched the job and where Sidney Poitier danced barefoot through the lobby after winning an Academy Award for *Lilies of the Field*. It's where Joanne Woodward waits unnoticed for Paul Newman and where Bob Evans was discovered by Norma Shearer. The Polo Lounge is where deals worth millions are bandied about while Burgess Meredith discourses on the merits of his late-life Oscar nomination for *Rocky*. And where a three-sheets-to-the-wind Henry Ford II, when he wasn't chasing minis and maxis, was playing pranks on Lee Iacocca by disguising his voice on a downstairs pay phone and waking up his company's top honcho.

Where the Burtons had an Oscar-losers' party but let John Wayne attend even though he had won. And where Johnny Carson was spotted on all fours, dragging himself to his suite, too drunk to make it upright.

Glimpses:

Leslie Caron wafting through the lobby wearing a gauzy, totally see-through blouse, almost causing a massive auto pile-up in the porte cochere.

Liz Taylor sunbathing in front of her bungalow, winking at passersby.

Tom Mix being tackled by an autograph seeker in the lobby.

Joan Crawford paying for everything less than five hundred dollars with one-dollar bills.

Marty Allen giving part of his Vegas routine at the front desk.

Katharine Hepburn diving fulling clothed into the pool after a game of tennis.

And for years, glimpses of Howard Hughes skulking around the garden and drinking alone in the Polo Lounge.

How does this hotel run, keeping some of the most jaded personalities since Caligula happy? Giving them privacy when demanded and publicity when sought? (But not bending the rule prohibiting picture taking in the public rooms.) Maintaining a sense of decorum and propriety (and maybe a bit of stuffiness) in the glitter-clatter swirl of Hollywood?

It's a little kingdom with pawns and dukes. There are employees who have been with the hotel for years, have worked their way up, and now need their own accountants. Others who have been satisfied with augmenting their salaries with a little skimming and scamming. There have been rivalries, nepotism, adultery, embezzlement, and robberies. Through it all the employees have got more than their paychecks. The fringe benefits include the vicarious kick from rubbing elbows with the rich and famous. Of watching them play, seeing how they are, knowing what they do after the doors are closed.

Knowing that Jackie Gleason misses the toilet bowl and that Harold Robbins's next best seller would be based on a Larry Flynt *Hustler*-type character. That Olivia de Havilland is a hell of a nice lady and that her sister Joan Fontaine isn't. And for all those years that Dear Ann Landers was handing out marital advice, she and her husband were sleeping in separate rooms—at opposite ends of the hotel.

And who cares, you might ask, and what does it matter? But it is fun, and exciting, exhilarating, naughty, and a little bit different, never humdrum. What a strange and wonderful place. You couldn't find it in Duluth, Minnesota, or Tucumcari, New Mexico. The climate's not right.

It could only be in Beverly Hills.

It could only be the Beverly Hills Hotel.

Chapter Two

It was an unlikely place to put a hotel.

For a long time, it was an unlikely place to put anything.

From its geologic beginnings, the place was jinxed. For starters, Southern California refused to leave the sea.

As other land masses, mountains, canyons, hills, and ravines twisted, heaved, folded, and faulted to sculpture the earth's surface, Southern California kept slipping into the ocean, where some modern pop prophets claim it belongs.

The best guess is that the Los Angeles area broke water for the first time some 160 million years ago, give or take a few hundred millenia.

Thousands of years later, at about the time flowering plants began to bloom, uneasy gurglings in the earth formed the granite core of the Santa Monica Mountain chain. The Santa Monica is a picturesque ridge running from Pasadena in the east across the Pacific, providing homeowners in Beverly Hills, Bel Air, and the Pacific Palisades with hundred-thousand-dollar, two-hundred-thousand-dollar, and one-million-dollar views.

Despite the granite core, Southern California managed to slip below sea level again. But some geologic divinity or another seemed bent on making it a suitable future site for Disneyland and Chavez Ravine. Consequently, an unruly volcano forced the land to resurface, where it has remained with only periodic attempts to earthquake itself back into the Pacific.

One other development occurred in the Pliocene or Miocene epochs, about fifty or sixty million years ago. Through some hocus-pocus of nature, oil was formed and trapped, a black siren waiting for silly men to come in search of her.

§   §   §   §   §   §   §   §   §   §

Fast, fast forward through time to Humanity.

§   §   §   §   §   §   §   §   §   §

It's not certain from where the North American Indians originally came, but it is known that Shoshoneans were in Southern California by the time the Spanish conquistadors turned their acquisitive eyes in that direction.

California was a newer land in a new land. Peru, Mexico, the Caribbean had been divvied up. Late-arriving conquistadors had to find new booty.

That explains why on August 2, 1769, the Spanish governor of the Californias, one Captain don Gaspar de Portola, found himself and a band of companions bedding down at a small river miles north of San Diego, at a spot where, according to all records, no white man had bedded down before.

The group bestowed the name of *El Pueblo de Nuestra Señora la Reina de los Angeles de Porcincula* on their campsite. Luckily for future cartographers and ticket agents, that was shortened to *Los Angeles.*

The next day's trek brought the explorers to a thick grove of sycamores with a watercress-lined stream meandering through it. They set up tents there, with no way of knowing or even dreaming that a century and a half later, other men would also put up shelter for overnight travelers. But the later one would have wall-to-wall carpeting, feather pillows and linen sheets, hot and cold running water, marble baths, a swimming pool warmed to seventy degrees, dining rooms, banquet halls, maids, butlers, bellhops, cooks, waiters, amenities, and goodies that don Gaspar could have imagined only in heaven.

This spot was called Spring of the Sycamores of Saint Stephen. No one bothered to shorten this before it was changed by its first owner, María Rita Valdez.

María Rita received Spring of the Sycamores in a land grant of 4,539 acres in either 1831 or 1841. (The grant says 1831, but the governor who signed it wasn't around until 1841.) Her name for the place was Rodéo de las Aguas, ranch of the gathering waters, in deference to the torrents that cascaded down nearby canyons during rainy season, turning a good portion of her spread into marshland.

María Rita tried cattle ranching. She shouldn't have bothered. As already noted, the place was jinxed.

Drought.

Indians (of the unfriendly persuasion).

Luciano, a cantankerous relative who, unfortunately for María Rita, was also mentioned in the land grant.

Their fussing made its way into the chamber of the Los Angeles City Council, which decided that María Rita should buy out Luciano—for the magnificent sum of $17.50. (The Harold Lloyd estate, a tiny portion of Rodéo de las Aguas, was sold some 150 years later for $1.6 million, and subsequently put on the block for $4.5 million.)

1854. An Indian raid killing a few neighbors two years earlier decided it for María Rita. It was time to get out. She found some enterprising Yankees (one, Benjamin Davis Wilson, got a mountain named after him), extracted four thousand dollars from them, and walked out of the history books.

Wilson and partners didn't fare much better than their predecessor. Planting two thousand acres of wheat, they reaped a harvest of debts.

Drought again.

More drought, followed by deluge.

Followed by more financial fiascoes.

1865. The Pioneer Oil Company began drilling. Oil had been discovered in La Brea, not far from the ranch, so why not here?

No oil.

1869. A pharmacist from Louisville tried selling seventy-five-acre lots for ten dollars.

No buyers.

By the time the Los Angeles–Pacific Rail Road ("The only double track to the ocean") got around to putting up a blink-of-the-eye depot, christened Morocco Junction, there wasn't much of anything going on at the old ranch except for some sheep herding.

The depot opening generated new hopes for the future of Morocco Junction. People were envisioning a thriving community growing up around the station, but people were envisioning a lot of thriving communities growing up all over Southern California.

The 1880s marked the beginning of what one writer dubbed the Iowa Influx. Incredible numbers of Easterners and middle Americans were making a lemming drive across the country to Southern California. Accommodating speculators and would-be developers tried to cash in on the influx by offering new "towns" for settlement.

These "towns," often little more than plats and titles, were popping up everywhere, even in the most undesirable locations. Undaunted, developers would try to pass off disadvantages as assets. Deserts became health spas. Mountain-goat slopes offered marvelous views. Desolate areas were desirable refuges far from the madding crowd. Swamps became harbors.

It was craziness, accompanied by freak shows, bands, elephants, and free lunches.

Between 1884 and 1888, one hundred of these towns were platted in Los Angeles County alone. Signs were put up for Sunset, Hyde Park, Ivanhoe, Border City, Chicago Park, Ferondale, Hesperia, Gladysta, Englewood (which promised "no fog, no frosts, no alkali, no adobe"), Ballona, Bethune, Minneapolis, Terracina, Walteria, Rosecrans. Only thirty-eight of these became more than a developer's dream.

Who, after all, would want to buy land in Border City, described as being "most easily accessible by means of balloon, and was as secure from hostile invasion as the homes of cliff-dwellers. Its principal resource was a view of the Mojave Desert"? Apparently no one did.

By the turn of the century developers began learning from their mistakes. A few miles east of Morocco Junction, a company using a fair amount of imagination and common sense decided that customers needed a little hoopla and packaging to entice wallets out of pockets. The developers of what was to be Hollywood figured that buyers wanted something more tangible than a watercolor brochure and a sales spiel. They were merely following the example of Los Angeles, which, as Morrow Mayo has pointed out, "is not a mere city. On the contrary it is, and has been since 1888, a commodity; something to be advertised and sold to the people of the United States like automobiles, cigarettes and mouth washes."

Accordingly, before the first customer was allowed on the site, the developers of Hollywood wrapped it up in a bit of hoopdedo and chicanery. An imposing bank building was erected; streets were laid out, trees planted. A hotel— the Hollywood Hotel, appropriately enough—was built, decorated, and staffed. To add to the illusion and effect, bricks, sand, lumber, and other construction odds and ends were hauled onto lots and fake SOLD signs put up, just to give the impression that a successful development was being snapped up quickly.

On opening day with flair and flourish, special steam trains chugged up from Los Angeles bringing buyers from the city to be met by brass bands.

The developers soon made a 60-percent profit.

This good fortune and success didn't travel west to Morocco Junction, which was still a train station and some lima-bean fields.

1900. More seekers of the black-gold siren, this time the Amalgamated Oil Company, bought up the land, brought in drills, sank the bits, and struck. . .

Water.

Admittedly not as good as oil, it was still a strike. Water was a marketable product.

Bowing to its assets, Amalgamated Oil changed its name to the Rodeo Land and Water Company and got ready to make a fortune.

And immediately ran into a slight hitch. The Rodeo Land and Water Company had a product. It didn't have a market. A few farmers, shepherds, and squatters hardly constituted a market.

It seemed obvious, at least to Rodeo's president Burton Green, that the customers would have to be lured to the market. He therefore set out to forge a community from María Rita's former ranch, not caring that it had been tried and had failed. Some people, it would seem, are made to challenge jinxes.

What kind of a town? was the first question. Green didn't want just any old patterned-after-Kansas City city. He wanted something more, something with grace and style. It was too much to hope for, but he wouldn't mind something with the flavor of, oh, Paris after Baron Haussmann had redesigned it with wide boulevards, lovely parks, and lots of trees. Green especially wanted lots of trees.

To achieve this, he imported a landscape architect all the way from New York City to plan residential areas where the streets would be lined with palms, maples, magnolias, oaks, and elms.

(Trees became such an ingrained part of the city's heritage that the city council was later to spend three full years haranguing, quibbling, and fighting over the choice of tree to be planted along Wilshire Boulevard. The palm narrowly defeated the rubber tree.)

Morocco was obviously too whimsical a name for what Green hoped would be a solid, affluent community. He scrapped it for *Beverly Hills. Beverly* for a Massachusetts farm where President Taft vacationed. *Hills* because there were hills.

1907. The subdivision was officially recorded, and Beverly Hills was ready for the great hordes who were expected to stampede toward it.

1910. Records show that only six new houses had been built north of Santa Monica Boulevard, a street running parallel to the stream-train tracks.

It looked like another bust.

The trees, the prettily laid out streets, even the water, weren't enough.

1914. Beverly Hills was so population hungry that when it came time to incorporate, it didn't have the requisite five hundred residents. The Rodeo Land and Water Company had to temporarily relocate some of its Mexican workers across the town line from West Hollywood.

Something else was needed. Beverly Hills needed the merchandising that had worked in Hollywood. It needed a come-on, a lure, a yo-yo in the cereal box.

It needed the Beverly Hills Hotel.

Chapter Three

It was an unlikely place to put a hotel.

There was nothing there and nothing to do except watch lima beans grow.

Burton Green's friends thought he was crazy, suffering from a failure wish, definitely throwing good money after bad. But Green was a gambler. He was an oilman in the wildcatting, pre-cost-control days of the industry. Big chances led to big payoffs. Green needed to take a big chance to make his Beverly Hills pay off.

Still, his friends warned him. Why would anyone schlep out to Beverly Who? when there were any number of convenient, fine hotels already built and established in downtown Los Angeles? The nascent movie colony had its own hotel in Hollywood, and Pasadena had the elegant Raymond for bluebloods desiring Boston in Southern California.

In addition there were several outstanding, and close, resort hotels that could boast of scenic beauties a hotel in Beverly Hills could never match. Although the Santa Monica Mountains might be cozy and nice, they weren't worth traveling three thousand miles—or for that matter, twenty-five miles—to see. How could Green's hotel compete with the magnificent Del Coronado overlooking the Pacific in San Diego or the equally beautiful Arlington, up the coast in Santa Barbara?

No one minded that these hotels weren't in the center of action. They provided their own action. Tennis courts, horseback riding, surf parties, picnics, hunting trips, "flora-and-fauna expeditions."

Edmund Wilson was one critic to rhapsodize over the Del Coronado. "Airy, picturesque, and half-bizarre, it is the most magnificent example extant of the American seaside hotel as it flourished . . . on both coasts. White and ornate as a wedding-cake, polished and trim as a ship, it makes a monument not unworthy to dominate the last blue concave dent in the shoreline before the United States gives way to Mexico."

Ocean or no, beach or no, scenic wonder or no, Green was determined to compete. He would create his own wonder; he would erect something grand and comfortable, gracious and lovely. He would plant his own scenery. He would build a place where prospective mansion buyers—his kind of people—would feel right at home as they scouted sites.

He would build a palace.

Nineteen years later it cost four million dollars to build the twenty-two-hundred-room Waldorf-Astoria in New York, but in 1912, in Southern California, it took only five hundred thousand dollars to build the Beverly Hills Hotel.

Up it went. Kids from nearby ranches rode over to watch the progress, open mouthed. Gawkers from Los Angeles braved the rutty roads to pass Sunday afternoons watching, open mouthed.

It was a sight.

The closer it came to completion, the more the hotel looked out of place, as if some pixillated genie had conjured up a fairy-tale castle and plopped it down where it didn't belong.

T-shaped, arched, cupolaed, its three stories fairly dominated the landscape. Soon it *was* the landscape, and the mountains and hills behind it shrank in comparison, becoming merely a setting for this odd-shaped jewel.

And the shape was odd, as if the architect couldn't quite make up his mind where to put the hotel and what shape to make it. It was designed in a curious bastard style whose variations have been called Moorish, Spanish mission, and Spanish colonial, although architect Frank Lloyd Wright chose to call it tawdry Spanish medievalism.

At best Southern California architecture can be labeled hodge-podge. Wright less charitably, but perhaps more precisely, characterized it as an "eclectic procession to and fro in the rag-tag cast-off of the ages." And why not, if taste isn't an overwhelming factor in the decision of what to build? Anything can be grown in Southern California, and anything can be built. It's the climate. So why not build a mini-Versailles if the fancy hits you, or an Italian palazzo, or a Greek temple?

When the Iowa Influxers made it to Southern California, they were homesick for their home state. They built small-roomed houses that "bulged out with a bunion in the way of a bay-window. Coming out nearly as far as the bay-window was a tiny porch. The Iowans had pleasant visions of sitting on the front porch in the long tropical evenings. They found that night followed day as suddenly as the dropping of a curtain, without romantic twilight, and that the evenings, even in summer, were so cold that they would have to muffle themselves in their buffalo overcoats."

Down-to-earth Yankee New Englanders, on the other hand, were not to be fooled by Mother Nature. Accustomed to the worst vagaries of wind, snow, and flood, they built their California homes with sloped roofs (to keep snow from piling up and causing a cave-in) and cellars (a place for the totally unneeded furnace).

The Spanish-Moorish-mission inclination is probably the most prevalent style in Southern California, however, thanks in part to a set of circumstances in 1915. It seems that the good fathers of San Diego, in a surge of chauvinistic mercantilism, decided to promote their fair city with a Panama-California Exposition. Let the folks in the rest of the country and world see the good life in San Diego.

After plans for the exposition were well under way, San Diego discovered that the good fathers of San Francisco were also planning such an exposition, the Panama-Pacific, with a similar theme at the same time. Something had to be done to draw people south, the fathers of San Diego reasoned, and with that in mind, they hit on the gimmick of designing all the buildings in their exposition in the same white-stucco, ocher-tiled-roof style.

It became a fad, a rage—everyone wanted a house with white stucco and ocher tiles. The entire city of San Clemente was nothing but acres and acres of white stucco and ocher tile. Southern California, as one writer put it, "went Spanish," although it was a Spanish that Cervantes or Goya would have had trouble recognizing.

The Beverly Hills Hotel, a forerunner of this craze, was built in the pseudo-mission style, with thick walls that captured the night coolness and held it, with a slight mildewy dampness, through the heat of the day. And it had large public areas—though nothing like the startling lobby of the Hermosa Vista hotel outside of Cuernavaca, Mexico, in which there is lined, side by side, a long, gleaming row of coaches and carriages, with plenty of room left over for busloads of guests.

In the Beverly Hills garden ten large bungalows were engagingly scattered. Most of the guest rooms in the main building were quite small, however, as was the custom of the time. The rooms in the bungalows were spacious and many, the living rooms big enough to comfortably accommodate grand pianos. The bungalows were meant to be adequate and appropriate temporary housing for people used to living on a grand scale, people like King Gillette (that's Gillette as in Trac II) who needed somewhere to stay while mansions and manors were being constructed.

The hotel had one surprising nose-thumb for the orthodoxy of the Spanish rage. For some reason instead of the customary white stucco, the Beverly Hills was painted a "Hey look at me!" unbelievable pink—a pink that at times is salmon, at times rose, and at one certain twilight moment, is the exact shade of the western sky.

The buildings were up, the plants were planted, and the stucco was painted, but it still wasn't time to throw open the registry.

Anyone can build a hotel, but not anyone can run it.

Green was a businessman, a Wisconsin immigrant, with neither the temperament nor the desire to manage a hotel. He was, after all, a rich man. Rich men build hotels, they own hotels, they stay at hotels, but they very seldom run hotels.

Green wanted an exceptional hotel. He needed a rare and exceptional person to breathe life and character into his pink jewel, someone to set the tone of the hotel and at the same time someone who possessed superior management abilities. The difference between the Warwick in New York and the Plaza is more than just the accoutrements and accommodations. It's the service and personality of the staff and managers, the little extra that makes you know you're at the Plaza and makes you want to come back, the intangible essence that a great hotel has.

Green went headhunting. But not far.

Four and a half miles to the northeast, between Highland and Orchid Avenues, there lived a very gracious lady named Mrs. Margaret Anderson. Mrs. Margaret Anderson was manager of the very successful Hollywood Hotel. A matronly, big-bosomed woman, Mrs. Anderson had the knack—the right word, the right gesture, and the right touch for making guests of many natures and inclinations feel right at home, as long as home was a place of luxury and service.

Green had to have her.

But his problem was, what did he have to offer? The

answer kept coming back—nothing but a big risk. The Hollywood by 1912 was established. Mrs. Anderson held its lease. A move to Beverly Hills, as her friends warned her, was nothing short of a move to the wilderness, the uncertain, and potential failure. All the reasons that Green's friends had used on him, counseling against building there, were used on Mrs. Anderson.

Green had to offer something more. He did. He offered Mrs. Anderson the managership, a lease—and an option to buy at a price that one astonished person said was a virtual giveaway.

Mrs. Anderson accepted.

§   §   §   §   §   §   §   §   §   §

November 1, 1912.

A lot of hotel owners suffer anxiety attacks on opening day. They experience an overwhelming fear, sometimes justified, that the doors will swing open and no one will step inside. One Caribbean hotel man had sunk a fortune into building a magnificent resort complex. He had spent weeks coaching, scolding, training his staff on the intricacies and specifics in the care and feeding of rich guests.

It was now the official opening, although a big party to which people were jetting in from all over the world was set for the following day. For some reason, all the merrymakers had scheduled their arrival for the same day as the party.

On opening day, therefore, only one rather fat lady showed up. The owner watched as three overeager doormen almost carried the fat lady to the front desk. As she was signing in, he had a stomach-turning thought. My god, the lady would be coming down for a cocktail soon and would be the only person imbibing. How uncomfortable for her. The owner quickly rounded up suitable-looking staff members, dressed them in suitable-looking attire, and planted them in the bar, drinks in hand. By the time the fat lady came down, the cocktail lounge was buzzing at a very convivial pitch.

She had a martini. She had another. She was ordering her third, when a second anxious thought hit the owner. The lady wouldn't be drinking all evening. He mustered troops again and transplanted some of them into the dining room, where the fat lady, sure enough, soon wobbled.

The shills had a very enjoyable dinner. The fat lady had a very enjoyable dinner.

The fat lady retired to her room.

Phew! That was it. The opening-day horror was over. The real operation would begin the next morning, but in the meantime, the very first guest had been treated royally and well.

The owner retired, clutching a very large drink.

Mrs. Anderson didn't need to hit the bottle on her opening day. It was a finely planned campaign, carried out with the strategy and tactics of a Nelson at Trafalgar.

First and foremost, the comfort of the guests was to be maintained. And there were guests on that opening day— one hundred of them who saw no reason to stay at the Hollywood Hotel if Mrs. Anderson was leaving. They left, too, along with most of the Hollywood's staff—Mrs. Hudson, the housekeeper; Mrs. Mary Parry, the linenkeeper; Wilbur, the gardener; Harry, the headwaiter—and most of the Hollywood's furnishings, which Mrs. Anderson owned.

The guests had breakfast at the Hollywood, while maids packed their belongings, and lunch at the Beverly Hills, while maids unpacked their belongings.

This was how Mrs. Anderson did things—meticulously, methodically, and well. From Day One, the Beverly Hills was Mrs. Anderson—dignified, sedate, ready for bed at ten. She attracted and accepted the Blue Book rich, the carriage-trade elderly who checked in for weeks and months at a time. These were people who "summered" and "wintered" and traveled with valets. People who disliked ostentation, deplored vulgarity, and expected a fingerbowl between courses. People who liked Mrs. Anderson and whom she liked.

And most important, they were people that Burton Green liked.

The image Southern California has projected to the rest of the country is of a dingbat place inhabited by suntanned beach bunnies, overmuscled weightlifters, and aspiring starlets whose average age (and IQ) is nineteen and a half. But in fact, the area has a large population of retirees; it's the Saint Petersburg of the Southwest. Green's plan had been to attract the wealthy retirees and near retirees to his hotel and entice them into spending their golden years in Beverly Hills, after they built new residences, naturally.

It began to happen, not overnight or even very quickly, but the rich came. They saw. They bought.

As he had hoped, the hotel was the magnet, a specialized draw that set the tone of the town. Hell raisers could go elsewhere. Beverly Hills and the Beverly Hills Hotel were Dignified.

In those early days the town was uncrowded and leisurely, totally unlike today's heavily trafficked chic. Early townies remember it as quiet, "lovely," and lonely, a place where a trip downtown on a warm Saturday afternoon could mean being totally alone. No people on the streets or in cars.

This solitude was to be expected, considering there wasn't much to the downtown—no Gucci, no Pucci, no Giorgio or Saks, just a depot, a drugstore, and a furniture shop. Even as late as 1924, the town was so undeveloped that on hot days, the few stores and offices in the central business district had to close to avoid heavy clouds of dust churned up by men working in the nearby bean fields.

To give an illusion of more substance and settlement, the city fathers planted a vibrant array of plants and flowers at the depot. One clump spelled out BEVERLY HILLS.

(Years later this flowery welcome was abandoned when mischievous vandals making an editorial statement kept picking strategic blossoms so that the sign read BEVERLY ILLS.)

The plantings went from the station, along Rodeo Drive, to the hotel, the same route along which the one-car trolley shuttled guests and domestics in the early years. The original shuttle was a rickety Model T that had to be replaced after an amorous Great Dane knocked it over. When the trolley line was finally discontinued as more and more people became auto oriented, the tracks were converted into a bridle path by Mrs. Anderson's son Stanley and several other scenic-minded Beverly Hillsians. A major attraction for heartthrobbing pre-debs was to watch the white-haired and stately character actor Hobart Bosworth elegantly ride his stallion down "Ye Bridle Path." As one of those girls now remembers, "Everyone came to Beverly Hills to see that man ride his horse."

Before long there were other reasons to come to Beverly Hills. The town was taking shape. Slowly it was looking less and less woebegone as mansions and appropriate landscaping sprouted up on the hills and less ornate, smaller homes were built in the flats, while the population went from seven hundred to seventy-five hundred between 1920 and 1925.

Something else happened to Beverly Hills, something that has made realtors there happy ever since. The something was called Pickfair, the house that Doug built for Mary.

She was Mary Pickford, someone forever saddled with the sobriquet Thomas Edison laid on her, America's Sweetheart. He was Douglas Fairbanks, the exuberant, dashing swashbuckler of the silent screen.

By all accounts, Doug and Mary had been in love for quite some time. Unfortunately, Doug and Mary happened to be married to other people.

It was a bit of a scandal.

Mrs. Fairbanks was having Mary over for dinner, unaware that her friend and her husband were holding hands in the parlor while she was in the kitchen.

The state of matrimony in 1919 was still holy, even sacrosanct, and divorce, to put it mildly, was a social no-no, although more than 150,000 couples were getting unhitched. Doug, intrepid as he was, got his divorce first. Mary was a bit more timid. She worried, or so her biographers say, about social reaction.

Doug was undaunted, however, by her reluctance, ever confident that in the end love would conquer all and the two would slowly sink into the sunset together. He went househunting, deeming it improper for Mary, once they were married, to occupy the same house as her predecessor, a little affair called Grayhall. (This was the mansion in which George Hamilton lived when he was squiring Lynda Baines Johnson to the Academy Award presentations.)

Doug finally found a great little spot at Summit Drive above the Beverly Hills Hotel, a hunting lodge that he soon had carpenters expanding.

At long last, Mary threw social standing to the wind and got her divorce, despite her husband's screaming that he would shoot that "climbing monkey"—referring to Doug, not Mary. On March 28, 1920, Doug and Mary, as the highlight of an intimate dinner party, got married in their Beverly Hills home. The press, it should be noted, dubbed the place Pickfair, and not the Pickford-Fairbanks.

A sign once hung in Hollywood, DOGS AND ACTORS KEEP OUT. That was about the attitude Beverly Hillsians held toward actors before the arrival of the Pickford-Fairbanks. Actors, it was widely known, were a shiftless, fly-by-night, ne'er-do-well, just-a-notch-above-vagrant breed that you wouldn't want your sister, your daughter, or your ex-wife to marry. The movie industry, after all, had come to Los Angeles to circumvent an Eastern patent trust and to be near the Mexican border in case a quick getaway was in order. Movie people were unquestionably a bad lot with loose morals.

But as the industry grew and, more important, made more money, it became harder to dismiss all actors and their kind out of hand. By 1915, the payroll for the movie business in the Los Angeles area was already topping twenty million dollars a year. The stars were making ten thousand dollars a week and more in those lucrative pre-income-tax days.

So despite the scandal, Mary, with her golden curls and pinafore publicity shots, was a "lady." As Adolph Zukor described her, "She was never extravagant, and she always appeared as she was, not as a big glamorous movie star. . . . She never cavorted with any boisterous society and she was not a spendthrift or a wastrel."

If Beverly Hills was doomed to be invaded by movie types, at least they would be the aristocracy of the industry, the ones who could figure out which fork to use first. The razzle-dazzle, big-deal-in-the-offing, lend-me-a-ten-spot, naked-starlets-in-the-pool movie people could stay in the baser atmosphere of Hollywood, where they belonged.

Despite the tinge of reluctance—a scandal, after all, was a scandal—the Pickford-Fairbanks was accepted by the Beverly Hills bon ton. The Pickford-Fairbanks repaid this gift of respectability by bestowing Fashion upon Beverly Hills.

They brought an extraordinary and enviable guest list to Pickfair. The king and queen of Siam, Prince George of England, the crown prince of Japan, Charles Lindbergh, Albert Einstein, Babe Ruth—all came to dinner. One duke, duchess, and entourage of seventeen came for a weekend and stayed for months. An invitation to Pickfair was an invitation from the king and queen, and their castle was in Beverly Hills.

Before long, the other movie personages recognized the

comforts and chicness of the town. If it was good enough for Doug and Mary, it must be pretty damn good. The city directory began to read like a list of top-grossers.

Gloria Swanson lived above the hotel, at 904 Crescent Drive. Rudolph Valentino was to move into his Falcon's Lair. John Gilbert and Ina Claire shared a manor on Tower Road, as did King Vidor and Eleanor Boardman, and John Barrymore and Dolores Costello (although the latter's house was more a castle than a manor). Carl Laemmle had his Dias Dorados on Benedict Canyon. Then there were Tom Mix's 1010 Summit, Chaplin's 1103 Cove Way, Marion Davies's estate at 1700 Lexington Road, Corinne Griffith's 912 Rexford Drive. At various times Greta Garbo lived in town, as did Pauline Frederick, Richard Barthelmess, Wallace Beery, Walter Pidgeon, H. B. Warner, Ramon Novarro, Hunt Stromberg, Clara Bow, and Stan Laurel.

And best of all, there was Will Rogers, whose divine intervention managed to gouge federal funds from Washington for a Beverly Hills post office.

"We're getting mail out here," he wrote to Andrew Mellon, secretary of the treasury, "and handling it in a tent. It's mostly circulars from Washington making speeches about prosperity and it makes good reading while you are waiting for the foreclosure. It seems you owe us $250,000 for a post office and they can't get the dough out of you. I told these folks I know you and that you wasn't that kind of guy."

The post office was built shortly thereafter.

§   §   §   §   §   §   §   §   §   §

In 1920, Mrs. Anderson exercised her option to buy. By then the hotel was not only a profitable business venture, it was home. In 1919 her grandson Robert was born there. Her son Stanley was taking over more and more of the nitty-gritty daily operations, leaving Mrs. Anderson the time and freedom to be the hotel's hostess.

Stanley was something of a wheeler-dealer, with fingers in many business pies. He was part owner of the original Fox Studios and director of the corporation that built Westwood, soon to be home of UCLA. He was shrewd enough to buy downtown Beverly Hills property early, and in his spare time he managed to get his picture taken with the likes of Charlie Chaplin and D. W. Griffith. Son Robert is also under the impression that Stanley was part of the original Green group that planned Beverly Hills but that he pulled out when no one would go along with his idea to model the city after an English village.

In the twenties the hotel was thought of as a country retreat. In 1926 when the University of Southern California football team needed a place to get away from the adoring fans before a big game with Notre Dame, they retreated to the Beverly Hills. (However, not even the Beverly Hills and all-American back Morton Kaer could pull the game out. USC lost by one point.) A local paper carried a photograph of the team posed in studied nonchalance—almost everyone with hands in pockets—in front of the hotel, looking uncomfortable. The discomfort was probably for good reason, since the players were all thirty to forty years younger than most of the other guests. If the coach wanted a quiet, restful place, he couldn't have made a better choice. It's unnoted whether any of the Trojans joined Mrs. Anderson in her nightly rock on the veranda.

Not that there was a total lack of action at the Beverly Hills. An outraged Stanley called in the cops once when a noisy nighttime poker game in the garage disturbed guests. The Beverly Hills police department dutifully sent out a marshal to investigate. After careful assessment of the situation, the marshal took the action he considered most warranted.

He anted up.

The marshal might have won a few pots, but he definitely lost his job. The city council, not amused, fired him and promoted the Beverly Hills bicycle cop to replace him.

Then there were the Chinese cooks, who from time to time indulged in the ancient Chinese custom of tong wars, knifing one or two sous chefs in the process.

The hotel just didn't attract the madcap, the flappers, nor did it want to. However, Mrs. Anderson did once give a dinner to show her goodwill to the community. The invitations read formal attire at dinner and costumes and masks at the dance afterward. One slightly illiterate debutante misread the invitation and waltzed in to dinner, a few minutes after everyone else was seated. She was dressed in outrageous costume pajamas, much to her consternation and the other guests' amusement.

The hotel was the center of a community that was insular and self-contented, although an observer, a longtime society reporter there, contends that "Beverly Hills people weren't snobbish, it was simply that that was their world and that was sufficient." It was not surprising, then, that in 1923 many of the fine citizens of Beverly Hills were outraged, dismayed, and more than a little agitated when a move was made to annex Beverly Hills to (of all horrors) Los Angeles.

Los Angeles was in an annexing frenzy, gobbling up one small community after another with the promise that as part of Los Angeles, they would be plugged into the LA water system. The original twenty-eight-acre pueblo eventually exploded to more than 450 square miles. Will Rogers worried that his home state of Oklahoma would be annexed next. The boundaries of the City of the Angels never went that far east, but it did seem natural for LA to take over Beverly Hills, which was being totally surrounded by newly acquired territories.

To add to the external annexation pressure, Beverly Hills was faced with an internal crisis. The Rodeo Land and Water Company wanted out. The profit in supplying water to its creation had diminished greatly for the company, and although it had a contract with the city, it didn't want to honor it.

Now it just so happened that Beverly Hills had recently hired a bright young city attorney, just recently graduated from nothing less than the Harvard Law School. And it further just so happened that this fellow had studied utilities law under no one less than the eminent jurist Felix Frankfurter.

Paul E. Schwab, this city attorney, assessed the situation and decided that Beverly Hills had a case against the Rodeo Land and Water Company. So he sued.

Now it might have been a coincidence—coincidences do happen—but about the time the lawsuit was filed, the annexation movement began. As was later noted, "It is Mr. Schwab's belief that the annexation question arose directly from his suit. Apparently legal council of the utility company had advised its client to encourage the annexation as a way around court action; if Beverly Hills came under the jurisdiction of Los Angeles, the company would no longer be responsible for its water supply. The company accepted this advice and in a very short time collected enough signatures to force a special election on annexation."

Election day was April 24, 1923, and the days before were filled with door-to-door canvassing of the town's one thousand voters as pros argued "annexation or stagnation" and antis countered that the vote was cheap ploy by Los Angeles to get the rich Beverly Hills tax base. The Rodeo Land and Water Company added to the politicking by hanging an enormous sign at Canon and Santa Monica.

On the morning of the referendum, Beverly Hillsians found bottles of putrid water on their doorsteps, along with notes stating that this was how the water in Beverly Hills would look if the good citizens didn't have the good sense to vote for annexation.

The dirty trick might have worked but for decisive action taken in the late afternoon. The "noes" formed a parade and marched around Beverly Hills with Will Rogers, director Fred Niblo, Douglas Fairbanks, Mary

Pickford, Harold Lloyd, Conrad Nagel, Rudolph Valentino, and Tom Mix in the lead. The stars offered free autographed pictures for every promised no vote.

The noes won, 507 to 337.

(Not unexpectedly, the footnote to all this is that today the water in Beverly Hills is almost undrinkable, much to the happiness and good fortune of the Sparkletts Bottled Water people.)

In those yearly years, if you wanted to do anything in town, you went to the hotel. There was always some sort of dance, party, or public recital being held there. The recitals were often lobby events. Sometimes the performers were local prodigies; other times they were better-established and even prominent artists who lived in town or were visiting the hotel. Estelle Heartt Dreyfus sang at one such recital. Estelle Heartt Dreyfus carved her way into immortality by being the contralto who sang at the opening of the Hollywood Bowl in 1922. She also rented a bungalow at the hotel.

Sometimes a nonprofessional guest was prevailed upon to demonstrate some talent or other. It was duly written up in the city's paper, the *Beverly Hills Citizen*—front page, no less—that one Miss Bathie Stuart from New Zealand was kind enough to perform Maori dances.

"Her costume was native, the skirt being of long strands of native flax decorated with herb juices so that it looked almost like beads. The bodice was of woven fibers, highly decorated. A feather cape was also worn. Her numbers included chants and songs in the Maori tongue and she gave a description of each and translated the words. The intonations and voice variations were remarkable and the music haunting."

Parties went from intimate affairs in the round teahouse out in the garden, to extravaganzas in any of the several larger rooms in the main building.

The teahouse was a beautiful little place that was usually arranged with a stage for a band in the center and tables clustered around it. With the doors thrown open on warm nights, and the lush scents of poinsettia, hibiscus, and gardenias drifting in, it was a romantic and very popular spot. Never open to the public, it was booked only for private parties, such as dinner dances, club meetings, and, in the case of Violette Johnson, a high tea.

Violette and her mother smothered the teahouse with her namesake flower in every shade of purple and invited twenty or thirty friends to celebrate her engagement to Fred Nason (owner of the Beverly Hills Moving and Transfer Company, a lucrative business in highly mobile Southern California).

In the main building were several rooms of varying sizes to accommodate just about all types of meetings, conferences, and parties (as long as they weren't brawls). The Crystal Ballroom, however, was always a favorite. This bilevel room was both intimate and large, and its red velvet and chandeliers gave it a charm and warmth quite unlike most hotel ballrooms.

This was the room where Howard Hughes furthered his off-the-wall, whack-a-ding-ho reputation and legend. At the unlikely hour of 3:30 one morning, the front desk got a call from Hughes. He had a very important conference to conduct, and he must rent a room. But not just any room; he must rent the Crystal.

"How many people will be attending your conference?" the desk clerk inquired, unfazed by still another Hughes eccentricity.

Well, there would be three—no, that would be four, counting Hughes.

"But Mr. Hughes," the clerk sputtered, now a bit perturbed, "wouldn't you prefer a smaller room? Surely a smaller room would fit your needs?"

Mr. Hughes was quite adamant that his need was the Crystal Room. So, at 4:00 A.M., Hughes and his three conferees filed into the room, where a small round table had been placed under the enormous center chandelier, and the conference began. Later Hughes told the hotel manager it was one of the few times he felt completely secure at a meeting, no doubt figuring that the walls were so far away from his little table that no monitoring device could pick up the conversation.

Samuel Goldwyn commandeered the Crystal Room when he wanted to impress the world with his style and generosity. He used the marriage of stars Vilma Banky and Rod La Rocque as an excuse to throw a sumptuous party there. As La Rocque described it, "Sam just took over the hotel. There was a magnificent spread. Somebody says it was composed partly of papier-mâché turkeys for display. The reception was so gargantuan, I guess the thought suggested itself. There was no papier-mâché, believe me. It was certainly memorable. It was so funny—we thought we'd be married quietly in Santa Barbara."

Besides being the party center of town, with only Pickfair as its rival, the hotel served as the community meeting place. On Sundays and Thursdays, the buffets were *de rigueur* because it was a place for everyone to hobnob and because there were no other restaurants in town. The Beverly Hills Women's Club held meetings at the hotel until they built their own place. (The club had originally been called the Beverly Hills Woman's Club, growing out of the woman's-rights movement of the late nineteenth century. However, in the twentieth century, members decided *woman's* was ungrammatical and changed it.) The realty board likewise met there, and on Sunday mornings congregations without church buildings took over the ballrooms in which, the night before, extreme secularism had been the rule. In 1924 it was so congested that the Episcopalians alternated Sundays with the Church of the Good Shepherd (later to be commonly referred to as Our Lady of the Cadillacs).

If the hotel was the center of the social action for the town's adults, it was even more so for the kiddies. One of the youngsters then, Cecile Morrison, née Woods, now recalls that the only recreation in town for those under eighteen was at the hotel.

There were tennis, the pool, and best of all, the free movies. The Beverly Hills had the only public screening room in the area, the next-closer being a hard drive away in Hollywood. Everyone was invited to the films. Morrison and her sister Helen would pay five cents to take the Toonerville Trolley to the hotel. Most of the kiddies, however, arrived in chauffeur-driven limousines. Baby Barbara Hutton managed to one-up everyone by bringing not only a chauffeur, but a bodyguard.

On big holidays, the hotel treated kids to events like egg rolls on the lawn and entertainment like Jocko the monkey. Christmases were the best times. In 1926 three trees on the lawn were decorated at a special ceremony with 175 colored lights. The next year an "ice palace" was put up in the sunroom, and on Christmas Eve a six-foot, eight-inch Santa Claus crawled out in time to light the tree and hear twenty choirboys from the Saint Thomas Church sing carols.

§   §   §   §   §   §   §   §   §   §

And so the twenties passed.

The hotel enjoyed profit and success. It was already an institution (it doesn't take long for institutions and legends to be established in Southern California), and it seemed as if its success, like the nation's prosperity and good times, was there to stay.

Chapter Four

The parties were bigger... the pace was faster... the shows were broader, the buildings were higher, the morals were lower and the liquor was cheaper.

F. Scott Fitzgerald,
summing up the Roaring Twenties.

The Roaring Twenties. The hurly-burly, Charleston-flapping, speculating, money-making Roaring Twenties. Good times were there to stay. Prosperity was as plain as the figures on the financial page and the Model A, with its gear-shift transmission, in the garage. The country's gross national product was rising, union membership dropping. (Who needed unions when wages had never been higher?) American goods were flooding the world, and new millionaires were being made all the time. (There were more millionaires—511—in 1929 than there were in the 1960s, when the population had risen by 50 percent.)

To some extent this euphoria was induced by the stock market, a national fad that could make anyone with the right tips and a little margin as rich as Rockefeller. *Get aboard* the speculation train, Hearst columnist Arthur Brisbane exhorted, and people scrambled on.

The fluctuating flipflops of the market were as much the talk of the town as Babe Ruth's batting average and the new movie at the Bijou. The market was on people's minds so much that when Charlie Chaplin mentioned that his blood pressure had fallen, playwright George S. Kaufman wanted to know if it was common or preferred. The Marx Brothers were getting tips from elevator operators, chauffeurs from their employers, nurses from patients. Between 1923 and 1929 the number of shares traded went from 236 million to 1.25 billion a year. Samuel Insull was able to parlay a gift of fifteen thousand dollars' worth of stock he received from Thomas Edison in the early part of the century into a utilities empire worth three billion dollars.

Oompah-pa was out. Jazz was in, and Zelda Fitzgerald took a liking to the Plaza fountain. It was presto tempo and getting faster.

But not everyone and everything were touched by these simply modern and daring carryings-on. Some people refused to raise their hemlines or bob their hair. Shocked or bemused by the Jazz Age, they watched from the side, wondering where it would all end.

The Beverly Hills was hardly a hotel of the Jazz Age, as hurly-burly was hardly Mrs. Anderson's style. Shenanigans were for other places. Her rooms, suites, and bungalows were always filled to capacity but filled by people who wanted shelter from the antics occurring elsewhere. And although some people sniffed that the Beverly Hills was little better than a retirement home, its accountants had no cause for complaint.

There were other places for the hooch set, anyway. On January 9, 1927, the exotic-eyed, Russian-born screen star Alla Nazimova, having free-spent her way through a fortune, turned her West Hollywood mansion into the Garden of Allah Hotel. Right from its opening, this hotel savored a reputation for being the spot where the movie industry went to cavort. One producer called it a place for transients—a glorified whorehouse.

Twenty-five thin-walled villas were tucked around an enormous pool, which was to be the scene of countless parties and dunkings. Once, Tallulah Bankhead, a lady who conducted newspaper interviews perched on a piano, legs dangling, her absence of underwear obvious, dived into the pool in full evening regalia, diamonds and all. Her long dress got in the way of her somewhat inadequate breaststroke. In order to reach the surface, she peeled it off.

According to Sheilah Graham, Bankhead then yelled, "Everyone's been dying to see my body. Now they can see it."

Swimming was not one of Bankhead's more developed talents. To keep the next viewing of her body from being in the county morgue, Johnny Weissmuller felt compelled to do a Tarzan. He dived into the pool and pulled her out.

The Garden was the type of place where an innocent early-morning walk past Robert Benchley's door—he was a regular there except for when his wife was in town; then he went to the Beverly Hills—meant an invitation in for a drink, and another, and . . .

For anyone seeking more decorum than was usually present at the Garden, but who also desired somewhere a little livelier than the Beverly Hills, there was the Beverly Wilshire, a large downtown hotel, modeled after a Florentine palazzo, that had opened in December 1927. It had nine stories, 350 rooms and apartments, six ballrooms, and room for eight shops. Supposedly costing three million dollars, it was touted as the last word in an apartment-hotel.

With characteristic beneficence, Mrs. Anderson attended the opening party there and brought along some of her own guests. She wished the new owner, builder Walter G. McCarty, every success, and he thanked her for "the kindly motive that prompts your congratulations," while the camera lights popped.

In 1928 it probably didn't look as if Mrs. Anderson had much to fear from this new competition. By all accounts her guest list was too established and too loyal. And in that time of prosperity, there were plenty of other guests for the Wilshire and the Garden of Allah.

Actually, many parties and events that had been held

exclusively at the Beverly Hills now moved down to the Wilshire. The annual Chamber of Commerce dinner, which got columns of publicity because of guests of honor like Mary Pickford and Jack Benny, was now held at both places, after pressure from the Chamber of Commerce. (It was at one of those dinners that Jack Benny received the title Honorary Dogcatcher of Beverly Hills. Reportedly he was rather piqued because he thought he deserved the same honorary mayor title Will Rogers had received a few years earlier. But to Beverly Hillsians, no one, not even Benny, was in the same league as Rogers.)

The Beverly Wilshire was the novelty, but many people still maintained good feelings toward the Beverly Hills, especially the Crystal Room. When Mr. and Mrs. Basil Rathbone threw a small costume party for four hundred, that's where it took place.

It was all destined to end soon. The prosperity, the good times, and the Beverly Hills' success were about to poof away. The economic time bombs that would blast the country apart were planted and ready to explode, and the Beverly Hills Hotel would be just another victim.

It's conceivable that the hotel could have survived the damage of the Depression, but for one thing. By the time the stock market crashed in October 1929, starting the domino reaction that toppled the nation's economy, Mrs. Margaret Anderson no longer owned the Beverly Hills.

She had sold out in November 1928.

1928 was a seller's year. People were running around with money to spare and invest. They were looking for properties. Helena Rubenstein sold her cosmetics company for $7.5 million, only to be able to buy it back a year after the crash for $1 million.

The buyer for the Beverly Hills was Hugh Leighten, president of a Chicago-based company, Interstate, which also owned a resort lodge in the High Sierras. The purchasing price was $1.5 million, half of which Leighten raised by going public with 6½-percent-interest bonds.

Leighten took over in December 1928 and immediately began making changes. Serving as his own manager for the first few months, Leighton attempted to change the old-lady image of the hotel, hoping to capture some of the younger crowd that was throwing money around at the Wilshire.

The changes were startling. Rob Wagner, a humorist with a little magazine called the *Beverly Hills Script* ("The Swindling Servants of the Film Stars! Our Low Aims, also Comment—Gossip—Fiction—News—Society—Business—Gags—Reviews") wrote just four months after the sale:

> *The center of social life was the Beverly Hills Hotel, which became a quiet harbor into which old and old-fashioned people of wealth withdrew. Jazz descended upon the world, but that grand old pile remained untouched by its flamboyancies. It seemed that the Beverly Hills Hotel was to take its place with the historic institutions of the country.*
>
> *Then, almost overnight, it changed its character. Where once the ancient hostelry lay hidden behind its sheltering pines and palms, it has suddenly burst forth at night in carnival splendor, its facade ablaze with a battery of red, yellow and blue squirt-lights suggesting nothing so much as Queen Victoria turned Follies girl, wearing a blonde wig and doing a toe dance in pink tights.*
>
> *Furthermore the whole character of the hotel is undergoing a change. Additions and fresh decorations are underway, tennis and dancing are part of its new life and everywhere there is evidence that its drift toward what the youngsters called an old ladies' home has suddenly been arrested, and that henceforth it will hold up its head with the Beverly Wilshire Hotel and the competing joyousness of the Hollywood centers of social interest. Shocking at first to us old timers, we realize that this startling rejuvenation of our beloved hostelry is but one evidence of a change that has been gradually creeping over our entire city, now made so dramatically apparent.*

The real shocks and changes were still in the offing, and they weren't going to be caused by red, yellow, and blue lights, either. But Leighten and most of the rest of the country were blissfully unaware that the bottom was about to fall out. The handwriting had been on the wall for some time, but no one bothered to read it, except for a few meek souls who couldn't be heard over the popping of champagne corks and the sighs of self-contentment.

Herbert Hoover, of all people, had warned as early as January 1926 that "There are some phases of the situation which require caution . . . real estate and stock speculation and its possible extension into commodities with inevitable inflation. . . . This fever of speculation . . . can only land us on the shores of overdepression."

The Beverly Hills, with its sixteen acres in a rapidly growing community, was no crazy speculation. Leighten happened to buy it at the wrong time. He happened to try to change its image at the wrong time, and he was subsequently caught up in a morass of losing the old clientele who weren't happy with the change and not being able to get new clients because of the economy.

Leighton had hoped that with a stiff transfusion of money, the Beverly Hills would be able to draw a new type of freer-spending guest. He had thought out his master plan enough that after a few months of managing it himself, he turned the hotel over to Leon Brooks, fresh from the Alexander Young Hotel in Honolulu.

What Leighten planned was to completely refurnish and redecorate the hotel. People's taste had changed since the Beverly Hills was built. They now wanted bigger rooms and suites and more bathrooms. The bungalows had been built that way, but a lot of walls needed knocking out in the main building. To encourage a crowd of tennis fanatics who were making the Beverly Hills their lobbing and ground-stroking hangout, a new clubhouse had to be built. And there were plans to change the children's dining room and add to an arcade of shops.

It was going to take money, but after the crash, money was hard to come by. The debacle on Wall Street not only wiped out investors, speculators, and dabblers, but it wiped out the confidence of the nation. People wanted to hold on to their money, and they weren't about to risk investing in rugs and furnishings for a hotel in Southern California. Hoarding started on a large scale. People with money started taking it out of banks and out of the country or hiding it in mattresses.

Six months after Black Friday, the *New York Times*, with some wonderment and a fair amount of naïveté, found that Americans had stopped buying cars, clothes, and other consumer items. People were running scared and saving for a rainy day that was rapidly turning into a hurricane. Businesses went under, defaulting on bank loans, and investment money became scarce.

Inevitably, the Beverly Hills Hotel began to lose money.

The longtime guests who were still around started spending even less on things like room service and meals—hotel operations that make the difference between profit and loss. And the free-spending guests that Leighton went after, if they had any money left, stayed downtown at the Beverly Wilshire. The only glamour types that the Beverly Hills managed to attract were people looking for seclusion, who wanted out of the mainstream.

When Garbo was feeling more seclusive than usual in 1932, she took up residence in one of the hotel's bungalows, confident that she would be well out of the swirl of the Hollywood social scene. And to doubly ensure that she wouldn't be bothered, she took all her meals in.

Her defenses were breached once when word of her whereabouts had reached some particularly persistent fans, who camped out in the lobby hoping for a glimpse of the Swedish actress. For a time their vigilance was to no avail; Garbo remained only a whispered-about presence that never seemed to materialize. One afternoon, one of the whispers mentioned that a car was being maneuvered into the driveway in preparation for a quick escape.

Garbo was already in the back seat and the beat-up

Packard was edging down the driveway by the time the fans got to the front door. It looked as if, once again, Garbo had outflanked them. Not to be denied her goal, however, one tenacious tracker hurled herself onto the hood of the car and flattened her face against the windshield, attaining that precious peek at Garbo.

When Clark Gable wanted to avoid the uproar that was about to follow his separation from wife Ria, he, too, checked into the Beverly Hills. Of course, the rumor then began that he was using his bungalow for assignations with Loretta Young, his co-star in *Call of the Wild.* As the rumor went, Young was carrying Gable's child and had to cancel out of her next movie.

Generally, the hotel was not attracting the type of guest who attracted other guests. In the twenties the moneyed, respectable gentry attracted the Mary Pickfords who wanted that respectability to rub off on them. But in the early thirties, the hotel had lost its magnetism, and it was foundering.

Leighton brought in one manager after another, but none could turn the hotel around. In 1931, he hired W. M. Kimball, a man with wide and varied hotel experience who had once owned the Hotel Springfield in Springfield, Massachusetts, but the ledger sheet kept getting redder and redder.

In 1933 the crisis was reached.

The nation was singing the "Starvation Blues." Foreclosures were averaging a thousand a day, and one out of every five children wasn't getting enough to eat. On March 4, Franklin Delano Roosevelt was sworn in as the country's thirty-second president, saying it was "the time to speak the truth, the whole truth, frankly and boldly. Nor need we shrink from honestly facing conditions in our country today. This great nation will endure as it has endured, will revive and will prosper. So, first of all, let me assert my firm belief that the only thing to fear is fear itself."

Interstate, honestly facing the conditions at the hotel,

decided it could no longer pump money into the failing enterprise at the rate it had been doing. Besides the operating deficits, there were still $731,000 in bonds outstanding. The 6½-percent interest had to be paid on them.

Interstate attempted to reach a compromise with the bondholders. It offered to pay 2 percent interest for five years on the bonds and 4½ percent interest for the next five years. Any profit made in the first five-year period would be put into a sinking fund to help pay the later higher interest.

The compromise, however, couldn't be reached, partly because many bondholders couldn't be contacted in time. Those who were, weren't overjoyed with the offer.

Consequently, on April 14, 1933, a Friday, Interstate announced it would put no more money into the hotel. The hotel was to close, effective immediately.

As manager Kimball told the *Beverly Hills Citizen,* "The original order was to close at once but on account of many elderly people in the bungalows, I succeeded in deferring the closing until all the guests had the opportunity to make arrangements for their care."

In relation to what was happening in the United States, putting one hundred comparatively wealthy, albeit elderly, people on the street in 1933 was not of tremendous consequence. The year before, 273,000 people were evicted when their homes were foreclosed. According to historian Caroline Bird, one-fourth of the entire state of Mississippi was auctioned off at a foreclosure sale in a single day. This was a period when urban families moved every two or three months, skipping out in the middle of the night on rents they couldn't pay. This was a time that Bird sees as having "more far-reaching consequences . . . than either of the World Wars. Nobody escaped. Every individual in every walk of life was hit."

Putting those one hundred people on the street in Beverly Hills was striking proof that no one and nothing was safe from the Depression.

Beverly Hills was stunned. The hotel had been so much

a part of the community for so long that everyone just assumed it would endure. The city itself had escaped many of the hardships of the Depression primarily because the entertainment industry was one that prospered in hard times. People needed something to make them forget their troubles, and Myrna Loy carrying on in satin and pearls was the very thing. So they lined up to get into the movie theaters.

On April 19, 1933, the hotel closed its doors, and every member of the staff of one hundred was let go. Except for a few bungalow tenants, the place was entirely empty—no gardeners, no caretakers, no security guards, no one.

The bondholders were quick to realize that they now stood to lose even more on their investment if the property was not maintained. A bondholders' protective committee was formed in May to determine what was to become of the hotel. The committee consisted of Robert J. Giles, a vice-president of the Occidental Life Insurance Company; Ralph Reed, an architect; and Ernest U. Schroeter, a lawyer who also acted as counsel for the committee.

Their first action was to appeal to other bondholders to place their securities with the Bank of America, which would act as a depository. Once enough had done that, the committee, with the help of the bank, would start foreclosure proceedings. However, the committee noted, they would have to receive a satisfactory bid; otherwise, the bondholders would take title to the hotel and "either sell or lease it by the opening of the fall season."

It's since been stated that anyone with a ten-thousand-dollar cash down payment could have got the hotel at this time, but no one with a ten-thousand-dollar cash down payment popped up. The hotel failed to open in the fall.

In December, the bondholders' committee finally had its first piece of good news. It had found a lessee in Frank E. Dimmick, described by the *Los Angeles Times* as a "nationally known hotel man."

Dimmick took a long-term lease for five hundred thousand dollars and reopened in early 1934.

It was like opening a brand-new hotel—one without a cushion of goodwill, one that would have to start from scratch in establishing a guest list and reputation. Dimmick faced the same problems as Leighten, but magnified. He had to attract new guests and train a new staff. His one advantage was being able to raise some money for renovations and redecoration. Not enough to do a complete job, but enough to start.

By this time the hotel was bordering on shabby and was in serious need of a lot of work. Dimmick began a little at a time. Some new bathrooms, some larger rooms, and what was to prove the most propitious alteration, a dark and cozy cocktail lounge in what had been the children's dining room.

Prohibition had a disastrous effect on many restaurants and hotels. It's often the case that the profits of such establishments are made from liquor and not from food and rooms. During Prohibition, hotel after hotel went under, including some of New York's most fashionable, the Waldorf-Astoria, the Knickerbocker, the Buckingham, the Manhattan. In the twenties the Beverly Hills hadn't been much affected by the Eighteenth Amendment, since its success had never been based on receipts from a heavy-drinking crowd.

So it is a bit ironic that this new bar was soon the most profitable part of the hotel's operation. It became a hangout, a den of drinking for Hollywood's original Rat Pack, an Algonquin West, minus the Roundtable. This hard-boozing group of cynics included, among others, W. C. Fields, John Barrymore, writer and journalist Gene Fowler, painter John Decker, Wilson Mizner, Sadakichi Hartmann, and cartoonist George McManus, with occasional appearances by Will Rogers, Darryl Zanuck, and sundry polo-playing chums.

A manic bunch of nihilists, they wouldn't have been allowed into the hotel by Mrs. Anderson (who had died in 1930), but they wouldn't have wanted to be. When they descended on the bar, which at first had the prissy name of the Jardin, they took over the place, trying diligently to follow Field's dictum that "since the conundrum of life is so hard, the answer to it must be hard liquor."

As they soaked up the booze, it was their pleasure to cast jaundiced eyes and remarks on the silliness and pretensions of Hollywood and on themselves. Will Rogers once chided Barrymore with, "Listen, great profile, there's many a Barrymore in the sticks behind long whiskers."

Their antics were as unpredictable as what they would decide to make their evening's conversation. One running discussion was an "I'll top you" on who suffered more in younger, leaner days. Barrymore won this tall tales one-upmanship with his poverty story of when he was a struggling cartoonist in San Francisco before the 1906 earthquake.

"My roommate and I were so hard up that the only asset we had between us was a fancy gold bridge in his mouth. When we were strapped, I yanked it out and slapped it in hock. The pawnbroker ate with it more frequently than my roommate, and on better fare. But when we had his bridgework, we set up a slick routine for breakfast. He would order pancakes and coffee, eat half the portion, and then, with neat timing, I would dash into the restaurant waving a fake telegram. He'd seize the wire and spring off frantically with it. I would stare after him dolefully, then sit down and finish his pancakes and coffee."

After one particularly strenuous and wet session, W. C. paid a visit to his friend Rogers, with whom he had worked in the Ziegfeld Follies. It seems that Mrs. Rogers had just purchased some very expensive and very fragile crystal goblets in one of the hotel's shops. On spying them, Fields took a healthy swig from the cocktail shaker he carried for emergencies, grabbed the glasses, and proceeded to juggle them at dizzying speed. Mrs. Rogers may or may not have been aware that Fields had been a consummate juggler in his vaudeville days, but she did not think highly of the impromptu routine. She quickly had her husband escort Fields back to his own room.

These were fellows who took their drinking and playing seriously and were seriously put out when any merrymaking was denied them. George McManus, who among other things created the comic strip "Maggie and Jiggs," came into the cocktail lounge greatly out of sorts one night. Some big, exclusive party was being held in the hotel, and McManus had not been invited. What to do? After a couple of belts, he had a solution. McManus hurried to the men's room, removed the PRESS button from the urinal, affixed it to his lapel, and gained entrance as a member of the Fourth Estate. The Three Stooges later used this ruse in one of their nutball movies.

The group had enough of a touch of the insane and bizarre about them, that people readily believed the legend that after Barrymore died, the pack stole his body from the funeral parlor, propped it up in his bed, and proceeded to have a party in his honor. They were supposed to have neglected to tell Errol Flynn of the festivities, and the legend has it that Flynn almost passed out when he walked in to find what he thought was Barrymore returned from the dead.

Even with this crew quaffing it up, the bar receipts weren't enough to save Dimmick's venture. Nor was the tennis crowd who made the Beverly Hills' courts *the* place to play. Pro Harvey Snodgrass had managed to gather a fiercely loyal and equally fashionable coterie of players including Gloria Swanson, Mrs. Ernst Lubitsch, David O. Selznick, and Mrs. Sam Jaffe.

By October 1936, the bondholders' committee was meeting again, and foreclosure was again the main item on the agenda. By this time the Bank of America was no longer pleased to be handling its pink elephant on Sunset Boulevard.

The bank assigned one of its bright young men—an up-and-comer who was going to go far in the banking business, a man who had already risen incredibly swiftly through the Bank of America's ranks—to either put the hotel on its feet or find a buyer.

This bright young man was Hernando Courtright, and Hernando Courtright was about to bring his own version of the New Deal to the Beverly Hills Hotel.

Chapter Five

A Hollywood studio could pick up this story about now.

Hotel in distress. If something doesn't happen soon, big, bad bulldozers are sure to move in. What's needed is a knight in shining armor (preferably one who knows credits from debits) to swoop in for the rescue.

Strike that.

In keeping with the Southern California locale, make it a dashing caballero à la Zorro, charging in and taking command.

Call Central Casting. Get someone imaginative, handsome, and able to produce managerial and money miracles from beneath his cloak.

Forget Central Casting. Get the Bank of America. Hernando Courtright was made for the role. He was all of the above, plus he had a background that would have made a studio press agent salivate.

You want a dashing caballero? Courtright's Basque-born mother was a descendant of the free-wheeling, Aztec-conquering Spanish explorer Hernando Cortez. There has been an Hernando in every generation since.

Want a little romance, a little adventure? Mama Courtright met Papa Courtright when the latter, an Irish-American cavalry officer, was stationed at the American embassy in Mexico City.

After the wedding, they moved to Coeur D'Alene, Idaho (okay, so not every aspect to a story has to be romantic and exotic), not to mine lead and silver, both of which had been found in 1882, but to cattle ranch.

Now comes the pathos. As it turned out, Papa Courtright was a bust as a rancher. "Father knew a lot about horses, but not much about cattle."

Hernando, a strong-willed kid, one who would rather get spanked than have to pick berries on his eighth birthday, elected to follow his Irish grandmother's advice rather than his father's example. Grandma Kelley's maxim was: The main thing is to go out and make money.

He earned his first degree from the University of California, Berkeley. The second was from the University of Southern California's School of Business, where in the good company of Fred Nason (remember, Violette announced her engagement to him in the hotel teahouse?) and Howard Ahmanson, Sr. (founder and chairman of the Home Savings & Loan Association), Courtright was named Least Likely to Succeed.

The dashing-caballero image dims slightly here as a bit of Frank Capra enters the picture. Out of college, Courtright takes a job with the "People's Bank," the Bank of America, at its headquarters in San Francisco.

The Bank of America had been founded in 1904 as the Bank of Italy when A. P. Giannini got ticked off at conventional bank policy. He felt the Little Man, the small depositor, was getting short-changed. Banks weren't interested in him. So Giannini went off and started his own financial establishment. It enjoyed some modest success until the morning of the San Francisco earthquake.

5:13 A.M., Wednesday, April 18, 1906. San Francisco was shaken by twenty-eight seconds of Richter-rocking quake. Sidewalks buckled. Streets cracked. Chimneys fell. And some crudely made buildings crumbled. The real devastation came from the fires that started breaking out all over. Firetrucks raced willy-nilly throughout the city with no organization or orchestration, and soon the blazes were out of control.

That afternoon, Giannini decided it best to abandon his building in the financial district. He had the bank's gold and records transported to safer, less flammable areas.

Nine days later, while other banks were in chaos, sifting through smoldering records and waiting until vaults were cool enough to unlock, the Bank of Italy reopened. It was soon dispensing Rebuild San Francisco loans from its new office—a plank set between two barrels.

The Bank of America, née the Bank of Italy, was on its way to becoming the largest bank in the world.

Courtright had a knack for making money. A knack like that helps you rise quickly in banking ranks, and in short order, he was made vice-president and transferred to Los Angeles.

His duties there were varied. As an afterthought, one of his assignments became the Beverly Hills Hotel, "to occupy my time."

The bank still held the bonds. In January 1937, with some financial jigglings, the bondholders' committee bought the $731,000 worth of bonds—for $320,000—at a foreclosure sale. It was a move to give the committee more flexibility and to move Dimmick out. At the time of this sale, Courtright was the bank's representative on the committee. A new manager, E. J. Caldwell, was brought in from the Hotel Roosevelt in Hollywood. Before that he had been at the Edgewater Beach Hotel in Chicago, the Kapler chain in Saint Louis, and a few lesser hotels in California.

When first given his spare-time assignment, Courtright was told to either sell or save the hotel. But after the January sale, the committee still owned the place, so saving it seemed to be the only alternative. Despite having hired Caldwell, Courtright found himself further and further involved in the management.

I used to get the department heads together and hold meet-

ings in the evening after my banking duties were supposed to be over. At those meetings we asked ourselves, "Where is the money coming from to make a hotel a going concern?" We knew there was no money in a few elderly ladies sitting around the lobby. Then we asked ourselves, "Who spends the money spent in a hotel?" The answer was simple: the businessman on an expense account. Little Miss Jones, left a small patrimony by her uncle, sits on her nest egg, but to an executive trying to close a deal for Consolidate or Vultee or Texaco, or to sign Bob Hope or Bing Crosby for a radio deal or an author imported by MGM to write a screenplay, an extra fifty bucks or so is a minor item. So, we decided to mix the carriage trade—resort business with a transient business to give us some constancy of income.

Courtright's image of the hotel, although different from Mrs. Anderson's, was one that she would have undoubtedly approved. Grace and flavor would remain to ensure that no skyscraping addition would be built and destroy the friendly, homelike atmosphere. But the hotel still had to be transformed from a money-losing duckling into a profit-making swan. And to do that, in the words of *Los Angeles Times* columnist Jack Smith, Courtright was "trying to wean out the age of lavender and lace."

The first order of business was redecorating. Dimmick had begun, but now the redecorating would be done to the tune of three thousand dollars per room. And there would be no Holiday Inn monotony, either. Each room would be different, using the talents of famous and fashionable designers like Paul Lazlo, Jack Lucareni, Don Loper, and Harriet Shellenberger.

It was Loper who designed the distinctive pink and green banana-leaves wallpaper. (The fronds are cut out and pasted onto white walls. The design became so popular that patches were being picked in the ladies' room. After several replacements, the management finally hung a sign reading, IF YOU REALLY WANT THIS, PLEASE CONTACT OUR DECORATOR.)

In the process of this rejuvenation, they discovered rooms and suites that hadn't been used in years.

In the lobby, pillars were removed to make the area lighter and more airy. But no change was made to the ever-burning hearth, which must have appealed to Courtright's sense of his Spanish heritage. The fire, which still burns twenty-four hours a day (though it is gas now), was a symbol of the old Spanish-mission hospitality. In the early days, missions were built a day's journey apart so that travelers would always find a warm fire and a glass of wine at the end of a long day's trek. Courtright was also to have a chain-of-ownership map of Rodéo de las Aguas hung in the hotel's front office.

The gardens, much of which had gone to weed, were replanted. Downstairs an arcade designed for chi-chi shops was put in. This was where Frances Taylor opened his art gallery. Although he did earn a fair degree of fame and prestige in the art world, Taylor will probably be best remembered as Elizabeth's father. The young starlet began her long and convoluted association with the hotel when she'd come to visit Daddy at his shop and sometimes pose for publicity stills. ("Frances Taylor's art gallery in the shopping center, where daughter Elizabeth, young M-G-M actress, helps him dress the window for an exhibit.")

Courtright soon realized that image making can't be done second-hand. It's not just a question of passing orders to subordinates. There is a need to be there yourself, for inspiration, if nothing else. Courtright was finding himself there more and more.

He was drawn to the hotel, and people were drawn to him. And why not? Courtright was a handsome, outgoing man, best described as charming. Years later someone was to say that he is "probably the best-liked man in Southern California. I don't think Hernando has a serious enemy anywhere, with the possible exception of Ben Silberstein." (More on Ben L. Silberstein later.)

Courtright, despite having no hotel experience except for having stayed at several and knowing what he liked, had an innate feeling for the right touch and the right style. He had a sense of what would work and what wouldn't. He tossed out the name of the cocktail lounge. *Jardin* didn't make it. The lounge was being remodeled anyway, so why not a new name? That new name became the Polo Lounge.

Polo was introduced to the West Coast in 1882 by Mr. Horace A. Vachell, a British settler and novelist. Poor Mr. Vachell was forever being teased for his strange behavior on the ponies and his even stranger costume.

"Say, Horus," he was asked, "why do you wear your drawers outside your pants?"

By the 1920s polo had become quite the sport to play.

It's been said that the lounge was named in honor of Darryl F. Zanuck and his band of merry polo players— Will Rogers, Robert Wagner, Tommy Hitchcock, Robert Stack, Spencer Tracy, and the like. Deering Davis, one of these polo players who became decor director of the hotel in the 1960s, remembered that "Rogers had his polo field on the top of the hill overlooking the Riviera Country Club. We would stop here at the hotel for a drink on the way to Santa Barbara, or to Midwick in Pasadena, where the good, high-goal polo was played. A lot of movie people were attracted to polo. Jack Holt was one of the early enthusiasts. Hal Roach was a good player, and Will Rogers was a bad player but a helluva hot enthusiast. He was the world's worst sport. He hated to lose, and he showed it. Darryl Zanuck played, but not very well. He had a good team around him."

By Courtright's recollection, however, and with all due respect to the merry band, the name was the result of a favor for a friend. The friend, Charlie Wrightsman, had a polo team, which happened to win the national championships. When Wrightsman puzzled over where the silver bowl, prize for the team's glorious efforts, would be kept, Courtright offered to display it in the cocktail lounge. Once the bowl was there, the Polo Lounge seemed the only natural name. It stuck.

As any good banking man would hope, Courtright's efforts began to pay off. The very first quarter after the bondholders' committee wrested the hotel from Dimmick in 1937, a profit was turned, albeit a small one of $17,335.25.

Just as Leighten couldn't have picked a worse time to buy the hotel, Courtright became involved at the best time. The Depression was ending, and whatever residue was clinging would be washed away by the war effort. People were traveling again and beginning to spend money to make money again. Businessmen were on the move, and the Beverly Hills was letting it be known that it was there to make their trips more pleasant, enjoyable, and fun.

Part of that fun was Charlie Chaplin having lunch at his table, table 1, in the Polo Lounge. It was being able to squint through the darkness at Errol Flynn imbibing with playboy Freddie McAvoy, who was invariably accompanied by his butler, George. George's function was to keep Freddie's glass forever filled with Russian vodka. And it was probably fun, if a bit startling, the time that Captain Horace Brown, a William Randolph Hearst lookalike who became Marion Davies's husband, decided to test drive his trail bike—through the Polo Lounge. He managed to test drive it out before anyone had the presence of mind to stop him.

The hotel's registry began to include bigwigs, presidents of companies, wheelers and dealers, oilmen, bankers. And they liked hobnobbing with countesses, duchesses, and movie queens. So National City Bank of New York would be there when the Prince and Princess of Tchokotck checked in for a shopping trip. Or the retired president of Socony Vacuum might be having a drink next to the Baroness de Kuffner, a perennial on the Parisian best-dressed lists.

It was an exotic list. From Katharine Hepburn to the Countess "Babs" Bonet Willaumez. When a cocktail party was thrown to honor this fashion dignitary, the honorers were the likes of Constance and Joan Bennett, Gilbert Roland, the David Selznicks, Cary Grant, Mrs. Jules Stein, and Miriam Hopkins.

The parties were again "A" parties, the must parties, the parties you had to be invited to or be socially stigmatized. Parties like Ouida Bergère Rathbone's charity ball in December 1939. Ouida (born Ida Berger) had been head of Paramount Pictures' script department before she married Basil. Then she became a party giver. The charity ball was one of her most extravagant but, as luck would have it, least successful parties. *Time* magazine, in its characteristic bitchiness of that time, gave it the following write-up:

> *The project was sumptuous.* Pièce de résistance *was to have been an Alpine scene re-created with real snow in the sub-tropical palm gardens of the Beverly Hills Hotel. Afternoon of the party the rains came. What with this disappointment and that, by 7 in the evening Mrs. Rathbone was in a state of nervous collapse and could not take part in the festivities. But her guests had a high old time inside the big, rambling hotel where only the jollification was wet.*
>
> *Everybody was just getting happily awash when the Beverly Hills police arrived to break up the crap game. The more prudish producers went home. By 2 o'clock only the drunks and the pretty girls were left. At 4 the fights began. By 6 the flunkeys were mopping up and sweeping together the fragments. Next day people counted their hang-overs, declared it was one of the best Hollywood parties ever. There was some question whether the party made any money. After the 1938 party charity was reported to be only $2,000 in the red.*

Two hundred of Hollywood's finest turned out when Edgar Bergen honored his dummy, Charlie McCarthy, after they both finished making *You Can't Cheat an Honest Man.* It was even a party that *Life* went to. The ballroom was converted into an old-time music hall with a row of penny-arcade stereoscopes at one end showing *Little Egypt* and *The Great Train Robbery.*

Big deal if movie stars and social mavens camping out for months at a time in the bungalows weren't the big spenders. They created scenery the big spenders could be drawn to and appreciate. Naturally, there was no guarantee, especially in the beginning of Courtright's reign, that the hotel rooms would be filled with exalted, glamorous types. There were, without fail, some in the Polo Lounge, but having more Elizabeth Taylors and Baroness de Goldschmidt-Rothschilds floating around the grounds enhanced the hotel's reputation. There were, however, always a good number of celebrities in Beverly Hills itself, for the very reason that they lived there.

In an ingenious move, Courtright turned the swimming pool into a swimming club, with an annual membership of two hundred from the community. The club owned the green and white cabañas fringing the pool. At one point actor-turned-something of a politician George Murphy and Robert Montgomery shared one. Silent-film star Anita Stewart had another. Hotel guests were members as long as they registered. It was a stroke of public-relations genius and one that further endeared the hotel to the town.

The opening of the Sand and Pool Club in April 1940 was celebrated with a party thrown by the Beverly Hills Flower Club. Of course, a party thrown by the Beverly Hills Flower Club at the Beverly Hills Hotel wouldn't be cocktails over chrysanthemums. It was more in the order of a three-ring aquatic circus, a fashion show courtesy of Saks Fifth Avenue, exhibition tennis, and *then* the obligatory cocktails.

Incidentally, the name *Sand and Pool Club* wasn't some cutesy misnomer. Sunbathing aficionados and fanatics find there is a qualitative, if not quantitative, difference between a poolside and an oceanside tan. Sand, apparently, is the determining factor. To keep everyone happy and brown, bright white sand was imported from Arizona for a special sunning section next to the pool. Courtright seemed to go in for "you'll never believe what they do at the Beverly Hills" touches.

Save or sell it, Courtright had been told. The Beverly Hills Hotel was showing definite signs of being saved. By December 1940, the profits had increased so much that Courtright was able to announce a Christmas bonus for the entire staff of 118, equaling about a third of a regular month's salary. It had been, he said, "a very successful year."

The Depression was finally over at the hotel. It had a "successful" year because of Courtright's pampering, planning, and efforts. And it would make more money and have more success, if Courtright continued to pamper, plan, and work.

His next move was inevitable. He once was to complain that Beverly Hills residents "never believe in our own things. We always sell something to a fellow from Des Moines or Cincinnati, and he turns around and makes a fortune." Why should some Des Moines bankroller with no sense of the hotel or the town come in and take over just because he had cash to spare? Why not sell it to someone who could appreciate and nurture it?

In 1943 Courtright did precisely that. He sold it to himself.

And a few friends. Nice friends. Nice Beverly Hills friends. An aristocratic mixture of stars and tycoons.

Raiding the top drawer of Our Lady of the Cadillac society, Courtright brought together Irene Dunne and her husband, Frank Griffin, a local real estate bigwig who helped to put the package together; Loretta Young and her husband, Tom Lewis, an advertising executive who handled radio accounts for Young and Rubicam; Will Hays, once postmaster general and later of the Hays office, opened to keep naughties from sullying the screen; Tom

Hamilton, an airplane honcho who had been with the United Aircraft Company and Hamilton Standard Propeller; Willard Keith, president of the largest insurance-brokerage house on the West Coast; Tony and Sally De-Marco, the dancing team whose tippy-tapping feet were famous in nightclubs all over the world; Verbena Hebbard, a society-column regular; Joseph Schnitzer, treasurer of the Hollywood Turf Club; and Harry Warner, one of those brothers.

According to Courtright, it was "one of those deals that come once in a decade."

Perhaps, but part of the package was the investors. They made it, in Courtright's words, "a good buy." Now it wasn't just staying at the Beverly Hills, where movie stars came for cocktails. It was staying at, you know, Irene Dunne and Loretta Young's place. And all these new owners had lots of friends. It just seemed natural for friends to stay at a friend's place.

Courtright handed in his resignation to the Bank of America.

§   §   §   §   §   §   §   §   §   §

Wartime.

Beverly Hillsians felt themselves the first line of defense. The president as much as said so soon after Pearl Harbor.

In early 1942 he stated, "Enemy ships could swoop in and shell New York; enemy planes could drop bombs on war plants in Detroit; enemy troops could attack Alaska."

"But aren't the army and navy and air force strong enough to deal with anything like that?" he was asked.

"Certainly not," was the answer.

As if to accent Roosevelt's words, one insolent Japanese submarine took it upon itself to shell an oil refinery seven miles north of Santa Barbara. Some damage was done to the refinery, but more havoc was wreaked on the nerves and psyches of motorists on Route 101, which parallels the ocean. An errant shell whizzed over the tops of cars on the jammed highway and blasted into a hillside.

The shelling likewise damaged the nerves of Beverly Hillsians. John Barrymore, for one. The Great Profile called Beverly Hills' police chief in the middle of the night to volunteer his pool for active duty. After giving the war effort much consideration, Barrymore offered to drain his pool so it might be used an an antiaircraft-gun emplacement. Although his offer was turned down, several pools were emptied for just that purpose.

Beverly Hillsians, like all Americans, had the constant liminal reminder of the war—uniforms. Soldiers in uniform were everywhere. It became familiar to see uniformed—armed-forces-uniformed—clerks manning the front desk of the hotel, men on leave or men about to be shipped out. People were not accustomed, however, to the uniform that paraded through the lobby one day in 1943.

The incident began innocently enough at a Hollywood restaurant. As was his custom, Gene Fowler was having a bit to drink at lunch. Each belt was increasing his anger toward Warner Brothers, where he was under contract. His abusiveness grew until finally, probably just to shut him up, someone at the table informed Fowler that at that very moment the brothers and their executives were discussing the writer's contract.

It was too much. Fowler drove, as steadily as he could, to the studio in Burbank. The devil was in him, so outside the conference room he took off his pants, carried them into the room, and rather grandly said, "Look, Jack, I want these cleaned, pressed, and back by three."

Fowler was sober enough to retreat before a pink slip could be issued.

The Warner Brothers did not care to be reminded, especially by someone on their payroll, that they had once been tailors.

Where was Fowler to go, but to his friend Gladys Parker, the cartoonist, for a commiserative drink? Now, Gladys had recently received a curious gift from a war correspondent. It was a Nazi overcoat, complete with insignia and accompanying paraphernalia.

Fowler, with probably no more thought than to surprise his wife, borrowed the coat, but on the drive home he passed the Beverly Hills.

He couldn't resist. After all, wasn't Harry Warner involved with the hotel?

Up he drove, out he leaped, in he goose-stepped, shouting that the Nazis had taken over Beverly Hills.

As ridiculous a notion as that was, people were still paranoid enough to take the drunken "Nazi" invader very seriously, and they fled from the lobby.

It was hard for hotels to keep chaos at bay during the war, even though few had Gene Fowler to contend with. Hotels, like so many other businesses, had trouble keeping staffed. They kept losing their employees to the Selective Service.

Getting guests, on the other hand, was no problem. The war suddenly gave jobs to people who had been begging for work just five years earlier. But the war also made it difficult for these people to spend their money. Industry and effort were going for beating the "Krauts" and killing the "Japs," not for consumer goods and services. So although hotels could now book every room, they had to shut entire floors because they didn't have the staff to service them. (Even in this 100-percent-occupancy time, some hotels couldn't make it. Not surprisingly, one was the Stevens in Chicago, the world's largest hotel—not surprisingly because the army had bought the place and then proceeded to bungle the management so badly that it had to unload the hotel to the Kirkeby hotel interests in 1943 at a great loss.)

Travel was haphazard and unpredictable. Some people were just staying home. Car travel was greatly curtailed because of gas rationing. Bus, train, and plane travel was perilous because the poor citizen traveler never knew when he'd be bumped for someone holding a wartime priority.

(One of the minor flaps during the war involved one Elliott Roosevelt, son of a certain president. Three servicemen, two on emergency furloughs to see gravely ill wives, were bumped from a plane by a number-one-priority cargo. The priority cargo, as it turned out, was Blaze, a pedigreed English bull mastiff belonging to Elliott and his wife, Faye Emerson.)

More than one unfortunate traveler was abandoned in some godforsaken terminal, unable to get home. As Cabell Phillips of the *New York Times* was to write in his *The 1940s—Decade of Triumph and Trouble,* even if you were lucky enough to get to your destination,

> there was always the gambler's luck in finding a hotel room, reservations to the contrary notwithstanding. Desk clerks were easily overwhelmed by the sudden appearance of a clutch of exuberant young officers in town on a three-day pass, or by peremptory demands from Washington to make way for an emergency session of the Nut and Bolt Manufacturers' War Council. . . . In some cities, and this was particularly true in resorts like Miami and Santa Barbara, the military commandeered entire hotels for long periods, using them as rest and transient facilities and even as residential quarters for men stationed at nearby posts.

There was a shortage of all manner of living quarters, as workers moved to big industrial areas only to find no housing. At the Plaza in New York, peacetime standards of gracious hotelling had to be relaxed as cots were installed in managers' offices to accommodate more people. The extra people were told, with regret, that they would have to vacate by nine, when the managers came to work.

The Beverly Hills was not overrun by military types. On the contrary, when top military brass were in town for conferences with aircraft executives, the executives invariably registered at the Beverly Hills while the brass were relegated to lesser establishments.

Not that the military never stayed at the hotel. In 1942, Private Pat de Cicco checked in while on furlough from Fort Bliss. Private Pat de Cicco did not check in alone, however. Accompanying him was his bride, Gloria Vanderbilt de Cicco. Furthermore, the private wasn't going to be a private long. He was on his way to officer-training school in New Jersey.

Like most hotels, the Beverly Hills was conscripted for war-bond drives. Although all the good citizens of Beverly Hills might not have been allowed to sacrifice their pools for the war effort, they were welcome to contribute their money. So there was usually some Buy a Bomber breakfast—for a thousand-dollar bond you got ham, eggs, and Eddie Cantor—or an annual war-loan aquacade. One of the aquacades starred Ann Curtis, a five-foot-ten swimmer who held seven national championships and nineteen national swimming records and had garnered the nation's top amateur sports honor, the Sullivan Award.

When it came time to open the area's USO, the opening festivities were held at the hotel.

These events raised hundreds of thousands of dollars, but all war-bond-sales efforts were upstaged in, of all places, Gimbel's bargain basement, where Danny Kaye was emceeing an auction of historical memorabilia—a letter written by Goerge Washington, Thomas Jefferson's personal Bible, and the like. One of the likes was the violin that Jack Benny had unmercifully played for twenty years in his act. Kaye received a bid, in a note, for the violin.

It was for a one-million-dollar war bond.

Naturally, the bid caused something of a stir. Everyone wanted to know who the patriotic Benny fan was. Even after they got his name, few had ever heard of Julius Kornfein, a Russian immigrant who built his little Brooklyn cigar shop into the gigantic Garcia Grande Cigar Company. A million-dollar bond was nothing more than a show of appreciation for his adopted country in its time of need.

The war was ration books, skimping, and deprivation, even for the privileged who frequented the Beverly Hills. Rationing meant making do or finding some way to skirt the issue, without making yourself feel too guilty about undermining the war effort. A lot of people were able to rationalize that the rationing routine was so complicated and capricious that a little cheating was necessary to make it work.

You needed a scorecard to follow the rationing rules and the new, superceding ration rules and the revised-until-May-and-then-we'll-go-back-to-January rationing rules.

One Office of Price Administration guideline went like this:

> *Blue Stamps in War Ration Book No. 2 are used for most canned goods and for dried peas, beans, lentils, and frozen commodities like fruit juice. The Red Stamps are used for meats, canned fish, butter, cheese, edible fats, and canned milk. You have to give up more points when buying scarce food than when buying the same quantity of a more plentiful one. . . .*
>
> *Red Stamps, J, K, and L may be redeemed through June 20. Blue Stamps G, H, and J are valid through June 7, and Blue Stamps K, L, and M are valid through July 7. Ration stamps are not valid if detached from their appropriate books.*
>
> *Each person has a Red Stamp quota of 16 points a week (meats, cheese, butter, etc.) allowing an average of approximately two pounds per week per person. Each person has 48 points in Blue Stamps (most processed foods) to expend between June 6 and July 2. . . .*

and so on, through bureaucratic exercises *ad infinitum*.

Even if you hoarded your red stamps for butter it didn't mean that after waiting in line at the market, you'd get your butter. There was none, primarily because the dairy industry had jumped at a chance early on to sell to the armed forces at an extremely high price. This left the civilians, ration stamps or no, butterless. Faced with this crisis, Congress gave the margarine industry special dispensation to precolor their naturally pasty-gray product to a buttery yellow.

Precoloring was something the dairymen had successfully fought for years. But during the war, margarine was extolled as a satisfactory butter substitute. By the end of the war a lot of people had got used to margarine and didn't want to switch back. State legislatures were pressured to allow precoloring, until only Wisconsin (the Nation's Dairyland) was left with white margarine.

Beverly Hills matrons, an ingenious lot, came up with a rationing circumvention, a slight bending of the Office of Price Administration dictates. The hotel's room service would receive calls from the cooks of these matrons, not guests but patrons of the Beverly Hills. The cooks would place an order—a popular request was for "pork chops, blue"—and later would pick up the raw meat at the kitchen door.

It wasn't an easy time for gourmets, as their namesake magazine pointed out. *Gourmet*, the magazine of good living, had the ill timing to begin publication just at the outset of World War II, so that its proposed articles on eating holidays in Provence and recipes for truffles sauces had to be put on a back burner. Instead they urged their readers to plant their own spice gardens, to help out China by buying almond cookies from the United China Relief, to substitute blue cheese for Roquefort, to eat more game ("Although it isn't/our usual habit/This year we're eating/The Easter rabbit.") And they extolled the delights and necessities of making do with California *vin ordinaire.*

It was a long dry spell for the nation's drinkers. Hardly had they been able to wet their whistle after the repeal of Prohibition, than they were cut off from Scotch supplies.

The various war offices never thought that getting Scotch to the United States was a very high priority. By 1941 the remaining supplies from Britain had been swilled away, and those drinkers who switched to home-distilled liquors like bourbon discovered to their dismay that alcohol was used to produce gunpowder. Which meant that alcohol wasn't going to be used to produce sour-mash whiskey.

The long-dreaded order came down in October 1942: American distillers were forbidden to make drinking alcohol until further notice.

Until further notice turned out to be June 1944. Sure, in early 1944 an experimental blend was put on the market—it was made out of surplus and waste potatoes—but it was $3.32 a fifth, and there wasn't enough to go around. It took until mid-1946 for Scotch to become available in any appreciable amount on American liquor shelves.

That is, except at the Beverly Hills Hotel.

As the rest of the country made do with beer (beer production was judged vital to the war effort—aircraft and munitions workers got thirsty), regulars at the hotel were imbibing good old 80 proof.

A good hotel man always looks out for his guests. Legend has it that Courtright, who is unquestionably a good hotel man, took a timely grand tour of European vineyards and distilleries just before the war. Included on his itinerary were all those out-of-the-way monasteries where monks pass centuries concocting wonderful liqueurs. He bought everything he could ship back, making a particularly thorough sweep of Rheims, the center of the Champagne district. These precious purchases were then squirreled away in every available closet and cellar and behind secret panels.

Despite Courtright's thoughtful requisitioning, the Scotch supply got dangerously low because of the war. Since it wouldn't have been right to disappoint his increasingly loyal friends and guests, Courtright prevailed upon Will Hays to prevail upon his friend Joseph Kennedy, who was the ambassador to the Court of Saint James's, to see what he could do to keep glasses filled in the Polo Lounge. Before very long (isn't it nice to have friends?), a good supply of Old Parr—not much of a Scotch, but Scotch nonetheless—was being delivered to the Beverly Hills Hotel.

Many elements go into creating a mystique.

§   §   §   §   §   §   §   §   §   §

There was a picture taken in 1948 in the hotel's Rodeo Room. Outside the floor-to-ceiling windows one-thousand-foot palm trees are etched in the marigold-yellow sunshine. Inside four people sit in low easy chairs in front of a low easy table. To one side is a wine cooler properly equipped with a wine bottle. To the other, a white-jacketed waiter bending to serve. In the middle of the picture, in one of those easy chairs, is Maurice Chevalier, smiling, lounging, comfortable. He looks right. The scene looks right. The picture looks right.

During one week in that year the guest registry included Beatrice Lillie; Lily Pons and Andre Kostelanetz; the Philippine ambassador to the United States, Joaquin M. Elizade; the Labour party leader in the House of Lords, Lord Strabolgi; Mr. and Mrs. Gardner Cowles; the ex-regent of Siam Prince Banoyoung; and a party of Arabian princes who persisted in stationing their burnoosed guards outside their suite.

(A hotel barber was called upon to shave the princes, an unenviable task seeing that the burnoosed guards first checked his razor and then carefully watched every stroke he took. "It made me kind of nervous, and the once-over lightly I gave him was *very* light!")

In the lobby, one was as likely as not to bump into such a mixed bag of people as Danny Kaye, Dorothy Lamour, Katharine Hepburn, Walter Huston, Sinclair Lewis, Edgar Bergen, Al Jolson, Raymond Massey, Miss Taylor, Evelyn Keyes, Paulette Goddard, Hedy Lamarr, Maxwell Anderson on his way to persuade Ingrid Bergman to appear in his play *Joan of Lorraine,* or Aristotle Onassis, who had spent two years at the hotel when World War II prevented him from living in Greece.

You were not too likely to bump into Van Johnson, the teeny-boppers' new heartthrob. He was asked to leave in 1948 when his fans became too boisterous, even offering the elevator operators bribes for his room number. Boisterousness was not allowed at the Beverly Hills.

Bachelors suspected of having a streak of the roué were consigned to bungalow 14. "We like to put our bachelor cottagers in 14," the clerks would explain. "You know, pretty remote from the rest of the hotel in case of any little rumpus."

(The original ten bungalows had been added to over the years.)

This was Hernando Courtright's hotel now, just as it had been Mrs. Anderson's. His vision of the hotel became the hotel. It was Courtright who instituted the high staff-per-guest ratio in 1943. For every guest there was the equivalent of one and a half staff members. It was he who instituted the policy of no conventions. The Beverly Hills would never have "Hi! My Name's Harry" running around the lobby. The closest relative to Shrinerstime it would tolerate would be a subdued showing of new Rolls-Royces in a ballroom.

"A convention isn't considerate of those who aren't a part of it," Courtright explained. "If you entertain a convention of fifty people the whole hotel might just as well be in it."

It was Courtright, also, who instituted the policy, whenever possible, of having an assistant manager "room" the guests—that is, escort them to the room and make sure they are settled instead of being taken there by only a bellman.

Before the guests got to the room, however, it was made certain that lights were on, windows open, and blinds drawn in such a way that the scenery had a chance to be properly appreciated. At night fifty maids were sure the beds were turned down and the guests' bed clothes laid out.

The guest was the thing for Courtright, and he took precautions and pains to ensure every guest's comfort and pleasure. It was Courtright's idea to build private patios onto ground-floor rooms.

"We thought it would be nice if we could serve guests drinks in their own gardens, where they could even have a sunbath in privacy."

But before he went ahead, Courtright wanted to make sure that the guests in rooms on the upper floors wouldn't be disturbed by noise from the patios. So he built an experimental private garden outside his own room, threw a couple of parties, and then checked for complaints. Only after none were registered was work on the rest of the patios begun.

Courtright's biggest expansion push, however, was the Crescent Wing, a four-story addition that turned the shape of the hotel from a T to an H. Although modern and clean, and minus the ocher-tiled roof, the addition worked and blended with the rest of the building. Across its side was signatured BEVERLY HILLS HOTEL so that anyone traveling on Sunset Boulevard knew they had passed the true heart of Hollywood.

It was a typical Courtright touch that he managed to coordinate his Crescent Wing's opening festivities with the California Centennial celebration in 1949.

In December of that year, a parade of film biggies rode from City Hall to the hotel. Harold Lloyd. Pat O'Brien. Ann Miller. Maureen O'Sullivan. Claire Trevor. Leo Carrillo. George Murphy. Monty Montana. Arlene Dahl. Victor Moore. John Mack Brown. Jean Hersholt. Alan Ladd. And at the front of the parade, no one less than Hopalong Cassidy and his faithful horse, Topper. So while the state flag was hoisted by the mayor of Beverly Hills and the Sheriff's Boys Band lustily played "I Love California,"

Courtright released a balloon carrying the symbolic key to the $1.5-million Crescent Wing.

Beverly Hills itself was going through quite a metamorphosis. In 1930 the population had been 17,400. By 1950 it was more than 29,000. One thing remained constant. It was a town of older people. 18,472 were over thirty-five and only 5,275 were under twenty. There were 10,544 fifty and older.

It was still considered an inconsequential appendage to Los Angeles. Courtright wanted to modify that.

As he said, "This town has begun to move. It may be immodest to say so, but I think I gave it momentum. I had to get people over the idea that Beverly Hills was a resort area, a suburb. We created the idea that Beverly Hills was uptown Los Angeles. Almost every concept on which we predicated the Beverly Hills Hotel has been realized. Beverly Hills is like Park Avenue or Fifth Avenue. We're sitting right in the middle of it—in the heart of Beverly Hills in the heart of Los Angeles."

Courtright's involvement with the community did not end at the hotel entrance. He founded the Beverly Hills Wine and Food Society and the California Chapter of the Chevaliers du Tastevin, he was a member of the Jurande de Saint Emilion, the Commanderie du Bontemps du Medoc, the West Hills Hunt Club, and the Beverly Hills Polo Club. And in 1950 he was instrumental in forming the Los Angeles Hotel Association.

Here was a man to whom both his guests and his staff were devotedly loyal. Here was a man who dressed in embroidered sombreros and serapes when he felt like it and in London-tailored shantung suits when he felt like that. Mrs. Samuel Goldwyn once said of Courtright, "The days when movie stars and other Hollywood people used to turn up in elaborate costumes and getups are pretty much gone, but Hernando carries on the great tradition. He's the last of the Hollywood pashas."

He really was right out of Central Casting.

Chapter Six

So who is Ben L. Silberstein, and why does he hate Hernando Courtright?

The *why* is classic soap opera, straight from the scripts of *Days of Our Lives,* and will be answered in due course.

The *who* is more cut and dried. It contains no dashing cavalry officer or Spanish swashbuckler, nothing much to excite a press agent or screenwriter—except, perhaps, for those occasional whispers that Silberstein was somehow connected with the Michigan arm of the Mafia in the early days. But then again, Detroit lawyers are always rumored to have been connected with the Purple Gang in the early days.

(Silberstein's son-in-law, Burton Slatkin, pooh-poohs this rumor as "completely absurd," saying that Silberstein "not only could hardly know, or have come in contact with, any member of the Purple Gang because they were born and raised in completely opposite sections of the city; in addition, Silberstein was a teenager and not a lawyer during the period of their notoriety."

Furthermore, Silberstein wasn't a practicing lawyer for long.

No, his early bio is really more *Fortune* than *Photoplay.* After getting his degree from the Detroit College of Law, Silberstein went into business, the real estate business, and he was good at it.

In 1933, at the age of thirty, Silberstein, with his brother Joseph, started his accumulation of property. Just as some people have a preference for collecting Park Place and Boardwalk in Monopoly, Silberstein was partial to chain-store properties. However, when a good thing came along, like the Universal Gear Works in 1942 or, three years later, the Master Machinery and Gear Work, Oxford, Michigan, he was not loath to acquire it. By 1945, when he bought the twenty-five-story National Bank Building in downtown Detroit—paying six million dollars for a property the previous owner had listed at fifteen million— Silberstein and his associates controlled thirty-seven other business properties. Ostensibly a broker, he once told *Newsweek*, "We were always in every deal. We'd occasionally take a commission but only when we had to."

Everything was a deal to Silberstein. The word punctuated his conversations. If you were going to be a good real estate investor, you naturally needed to keep your sensors tuned for good deals. Never could tell when one might materialize magically in the mist—or the smog.

Which brings us to a more engaging setting than Detroit. It brings us and Ben L. Silberstein to Beverly Hills, but not to the Beverly Hills Hotel. It was the early fifties. Silberstein was planning a visit there, but even though it should have been an off season, the hotel was booked. Silberstein couldn't get a reservation.

Click. Click. Bing.

Dollar signs flashed up. Silberstein made a mental note to check out this hotel which was booked solidly during a slow period. Who knew? It might be a good deal.

Silberstein was no stranger to the hotel business, at least not to the buying-selling-speculating end of the business. At one point, he had owned the Pantalind in Grand Rapids, Michigan. At another, he had considered acquiring the Hotel Pierre in New York. (He passed on that after deciding that the city's rent controls would stifle profits.)

This Beverly Hills whetted his interest. On his next trip

to the West Coast, accompanied by his wife, Gertrude, and his two daughters, Muriel and Seema, Silberstein managed to get rooms. He liked what he got. And he liked what he saw. And so did eighteen-year-old Muriel.

"Daddy," she is supposed to have said, "you buy everything else. If you want me to be interested in your business, why don't you buy this hotel?"

Why not? It was at least worth approaching the owners.

A feeler went out. What would they consider to sell the hotel?

An answer came back.

They would consider no price. The Beverly Hills was not for sale. Period.

It was an emphatic enough answer for Silberstein to drop the matter.

A year passes. It's fall 1953, in Detroit. Silberstein is taking care of business, when an associate asks for a loan. More as a personal favor than anything else, Silberstein gives him the money.

The business associate is properly appreciative: "If there's anything I can do for you," etc., etc.

Well, yes, as a matter of fact, there is something.

Silberstein remembered that the associate had a friend who had a friend who happened to be none other than Dr. Francis Griffin, Irene Dunne's husband. Both were members of the syndicate that owned the Beverly Hills Hotel. The hotel that wasn't for sale. Period.

Sometimes periods, with the help of friends and friends of friends, can be transformed into ellipses or commas or question marks. Silberstein asked the associate if his friend might be able to encourage Dr. Griffin to at least talk with Silberstein.

Surprise, surprise. Not only would Dr. Griffin talk, but he sent back a price.

Five and one-half million dollars.

Outrageous, but a price.

The question was, however, why the price at all? What

had happened between the initial feeler and this one? Had the San Andreas Fault shifted to directly under the Beverly Hills? Had the palm trees contracted a rare blight that made starlets break out in hives and men earning more than fifty thousand a year impotent? Was the hotel about to be condemned to make room for another freeway?

Or was Conrad Hilton coming to town?

Hilton. A name to strike fear into the heart of any competitor's accountant. Next to Cesar Ritz, his name more than any other meant hotel. His worldwide chain was so vast and widely known that it was half-expected that the first astronauts on the moon would find a Lunar Hilton already there.

Word was out. Hilton was unloading the Plaza in New York, which he had owned since 1943, so that he might build a 12-million-dollar luxury hotel in Beverly Hills. Though many of Hilton's hotels have a sameness that leaves people wondering if they are in the Far East or the Midwest, he did have a flair for publicity and attracting guests. Hilton was the type of operator who, when he wanted to restore the Plaza to its stature as an in place with young society types, hired Prince Serge Obolensky, who not only made the columns in his own right but also had been married to John Jacob Astor's daughter. It was a cinch that with Obolensky at the Plaza, society types would return, and they did.

Would Hilton manage to kidnap the Beverly Hills' clientele?

The specter of the new hotel didn't exactly overwhelm the Beverly Hills Hotel's syndicate, but it did make them pause, at least long enough to listen to this man from Detroit who seemed so terribly interested in their lovely little investment. Tell him five and a half million and see what he does.

What Silberstein did was fly out to Beverly Hills to take a closer look, as any good businessman would. He checked out the buildings. He checked out the operation. He checked out the books. He checked out other hotels in the area. He checked out the gardens and figured there was "about a million bucks' worth of landscaping here. It took half a century for those palm trees to grow. You just can't put them in that way today."

No matter how he added, subtracted, multiplied, or divided, he kept coming up with a million dollars a year gross, easy.

And yet, five and a half million was outrageous.

Negotiation time.

Representatives from the two sides, seven in all, sequestered themselves, haggling and higgling for three days, but the bottom line kept reading five and a half million dollars.

Impasse. It was time for Silberstein to step in.

More haggly-higgly and impasse.

The price was the same.

Silberstein said later that those dollar signs in his eyes must have been shining too brightly. The syndicate representatives knew he would give in.

He did.

Those in the know thought it was a stupid deal. But then again, those in the know thought it was stupid deal for Burton Green and Mrs. Anderson.

"When we bought it for five and a half million," Silberstein said, "everyone said I was nuts. William Zeckendorf and the twenty other guys who buy properties all figured it was a mad deal. Those wise guys said I went overboard."

Of course, the wise guys had no way of divining the awesome California land boom of the 70s, when the hotel's sixteen acres would be worth an Arab oil well or two, say about twenty milion—nor would those interested only in buying and selling suspect the bewitchery of the hotel, the enchantment that transforms it from an investment, a mere piece of property, into a domain, a principality, a kingdom.

Besides, Silberstein wasn't frightened by the Hilton

bugaboo. No matter what Hilton built, it couldn't match the tranquil beauty and exotic reputation of the Beverly Hills. Silberstein was bullish on Southern California and saw the hotel as being "as good as Southern California," no matter what the competition.

§   §   §   §   §   §   §   §   §   §

January 23, 1954.

Announcement time. The *Los Angeles Times* carried this notice:

> *Hernando Courtright, president and general manager of the Beverly Hills Hotel Corp. announced yesterday that Ben L. Silberstein, Detroit investor and real estate owner, has acquired a substantial stock position in the hotel company. . . .*
>
> *Courtright will continue to operate the Beverly Hills Hotel as president and general manager and "all policies that have brought the hotel international recognition will be continued."*

So there it was, in black and white and the *LA Times*. By the time the sale was final, Ben L. Silberstein and his two daughters would own 80 percent of the privately owned and closely held Beverly Hills Corporation. Some of the other original investors included prominent Detroiters—Mrs. Eugene Arnfeld, Norman Hayden, Sidney Weissman, Mrs. Anna Srere, Donald Krotkin, Louis Blumberg, Mrs. Irving Blumberg. Names that meant something in Detroit, but hardly names with the magic of Irene Dunne and Loretta Young, or even Verbena Hebbard. Here was the "fellow from Des Moines or Cincinnati" that Courtright complained Beverly Hillsians sell to and then "he turns around and makes a fortune."

Not that Courtright's syndicate had done so badly. According to him, the return on their investment was a hundred to one.

As it turned out, the Hilton challenge never

materialized. The banquet business at the Beverly Hills fell off for the first ninety days after the Beverly Hilton opened, but even that picked up.

Silberstein and Courtright hadn't passively awaited the Hilton onslaught. At the end of June 1954, the Beverly Hills Corporation filed a suit in California Superior Court. It may have been competition, *per se,* the Beverly Hills Corporation didn't like, but that wasn't much of a ground for a suit. After all, competition is the American way. It is a good, wholesome virtue that keeps the nation in vigorous health. But unfair competition, that's nasty and vile—unless you can get away with it. Getting away with it is also the American way.

Courtright and Silberstein's complaint charged that the very name *Beverly Hilton* was unfair competition. The name, they contended, would cause "confusion and conflict" in the minds of people who might check into the Beverly Hilton thinking it was the Beverly Hills. The name *Beverly Hilton,* they said, would "mislead and deceive the public" and be an infringement of the rights of the Beverly Hills Hotel Corporation.

It was a nice try, and it had the Hilton lawyers working overtime for a few months. When they filed their answer in August, eighteen affidavits were submitted, some as long as one hundred pages. Their contention was simple enough. *Beverly* was a geographical name, like *Beverly Hills.* And Mr. Hilton *always* named his hotels the same way, the location and his name—as in Havana Hilton. Hence, Beverly Hilton. Further, they showed 147 telephone directory listings with the word *Beverly* in them. Of those, five were hotels.

Logic prevailed. Superior Court Judge Allen T. Lynch ruled in Hilton's favor—a geographical name could not be copyrighted.

The Beverly Hilton opened in August 1954. It was built on a busy corner where Wilshire and Santa Monica Boulevards meet, where there had once been a nursery and later a "sock 'em" golf range. It was the star of the Hilton empire, but it was never in the same league as the Beverly Hills.

§   §   §   §   §   §   §   §   §   §

Meanwhile, back at Silberstein's empire, court intrigue was brewing.

The stone-eyed, thin-lipped businessman with a penchant for pungent cigars was being captivated by his newest purchase. He was succumbing to the charm of the Pink Palace. Not that that meant a total change in character and loss of pragmatism. Silberstein saw the hotel as a truly big moneymaker, not just a tidy profit turner.

"The opportunities to improve its operation" were great, he said.

As he was to remember it, "For ninety days after I purchased the hotel, I made a personal survey of every department and came up with a program of improvement. I decided that the hotel, to maintain its great charm, had to remain small. We had to improve on what we had— make it the best. We believe there are enough people who want the best and will pay for it.

"The hotel was basically in poor physical condition. The main building was forty years old, the plumbing and wiring were in bad shape, and the furnishings were second-rate."

Translation: Silberstein was to go in and do what every hotelman with a bit of money does on acquiring an older hotel—he was going to spend a bit of that money fixing it up. Leighten had wanted to do that. Dimmick had tried. Courtright had continued. Silberstein's contribution was a program that would put all the profits back into the place for a decade. By 1964, five million dollars had been spent on physical improvements and about one million on new furnishings.

The ancient and willful plumbing was replaced with

modern sinks, tubs, and showers. Rooms were redecorated. New wiring was installed, as was a new heating system. The kitchen got new equipment, and air conditioning was installed.

(Air conditioning was a problem for one esteemed guest, but it gave the hotel a chance to show off how it cared for and pampered its clientele. General Sarnoff of RCA was the guest. He had a liking for suite 486. Naturally, the hotel made sure that 486 was always available when the general arrived. The thing was, however, that General Sarnoff also had a liking for air conditioning, and suite 486, though very nice in every other respect, was lacking that. So shortly before he checked in, special 220-volt lines had to be run into the suite and an air conditioner installed. At the same time the television normally in the room was taken out and replaced with an RCA model, one bought solely to make the general happy.)

Silberstein also remembers "intensifying the services, replacing the people who weren't doing a first-rate job. Our employees must be cordial but not intimate—they must anticipate the services of a guest."

The hotel was already service intensive. But it was to become more so. The basic Courtright approach, that of a cater-to-the-guest, transient country club, was left untouched, but touches such as French service in the dining room were introduced.

If Silberstein's bio had continued to read like the financial page, his war with Courtright would have occurred over something like cutting back on room-service waiters, or welcoming conventioneers to boost the occupancy rate, or decreasing the ratio of booze to ice in the cocktails— some dollars-and-cents issue. But Silberstein was no longer in Detroit; he was in Beverly Hills, at the Beverly Hills Hotel, where you expect life to be spicier, less mundane. And in this case you aren't disappointed.

Drama, melodrama even, enters the life of Ben L. Silberstein.

Ben L. Silberstein, you might recall, had a wife, the one who accompanied him on that fateful trip to Southern California with his two daughters. Being in his fifties, Silberstein was a bit past the male midlife-crisis age, so it must have been Southern California air, known for causing all sorts of aberrations.

In any case, Detroit wife didn't make the transition to Beverly Hills. The divorce was one of those long-drawn-out struggles that put attorneys into new tax brackets. Through it all, even after Silberstein had packed up and moved out completely, he continued to send home his dirty shirts. He liked the way his wife's maids did the laundry. Under Silberstein, the laundry at the Beverly Hills was to become remarkably good. Silberstein had expensive shirts, and when his ex-wife wouldn't wash them, the hotel valet had to take over.

§ § § § § § § § § §

Hernando Courtright, too, had a wife, Rosalind. Rosalind was a nightclub singer, pushing her career in far-flung cities, and she wasn't at the hotel when Silberstein moved in.

They met on a mundane mission—some papers had to be signed. Who knows why or precisely how these things happen? But *zappo!* something did.

Soon Rosalind was spending more time with Ben than with Hernando, with whom things hadn't been quite right for a while anyway. Here were two entirely different men, with only one thing in common, the hotel—one thing, that is, before Rosalind.

Courtright was a bon vivant, charming, outgoing, a horseman, a gourmet, who not so much hobnobbed with society as society hobnobbed with him. Silberstein was closer to the chest, someone who laid down orders to the hotel staff that he was never to be addressed by his full name, never, *Mr. Silberstein.* Always, *Mr. S.* He didn't want guests to know who he was and what he owned. A guest asking the switchboard operator for Mr. Silberstein isn't put through.

Courtright was a host, a man who enjoyed his guests, someone who followed the maxim the customer is always right until proven guilty. Silberstein, on the other hand, is the master, the king who carefully guards his domain from invasions by undesirable non–Beverly Hills types.

The story is told of the time two young record producers, staying at the hotel, were talking with some disheveled and denimed friends in the lobby (one of whom was barefooted). They were incongruous interlopers. Silberstein spotted them and ordered a bellman to throw the rabble out.

The record producers demurred. They were, after all, guests of the hotel, and who was this man to give them orders?

The man explained that he was the owner of the Beverly Hills Hotel and that they were, from that moment, *personae non gratae.*

We're not leaving, said the producers, but we are calling our lawyer, mentioning a very recognizable name.

Round one went to the record producers. They were allowed to stay. But something happened to their service— they no longer got the "Beverly Hills Treatment." In fact, life became unpleasant for them. The producers endured a few days, to make a point, then checked out for a more hospitable climate.

Silberstein's volatility can be triggered for less obvious reasons. A movie producer, a gentleman who had been at the hotel many times, was swimming in the pool. Silberstein happened to walk by—he walks religiously since so many of his friends died from heart attacks. His temper appeared suddenly, with no forewarning. The producer was doing something objectionable, or had done something objectionable, or perhaps . . . No matter. Silberstein wanted him out of the pool and out of the hotel. Under the circumstances, the producer saw no reason to stay.

Courtright and Silberstein are men of contrasting styles.

Contrasting styles with the staff. Courtright would give his wine steward a silver sommelier cup as a gift; Silberstein chooses to remain distant. One night auditor worked at the hotel for four years without receiving a single *hello* from Mr. S. On the other hand, it was Silberstein who instituted a system of semi-yearly bonuses, one July 1, the other December 25.

Contrasting styles. Courtright almost postured in his costuming. Silberstein, who wears old pants and knit shirts, dresses for himself and not for show. He sits at his Polo Lounge table, fourth from the left against the wall, unnoticed, quiet, watching. Courtright wants to be noticed, to greet, to have his name emblazoned across ads, menus, matchbooks.

It's not that Silberstein is never gracious and charming. He can take a liking to someone, like British actor Michael York and his wife, and order that they "be given anything they want." (As long as they pay for it. Silberstein believes in giving his guests everything they pay for. No more. But emphatically no less.)

Which does not mean to say Silberstein is an ungenerous man. Recently he gave a $150,000 Maillol sculpture to the Detroit Museum of Art and contributed $250,000 in his children's names to establish a pain clinic at Wayne State University. He gave the same amount to the UCLA Medical School.

They were very different men, Courtright and Silberstein. In temperament. In style. One of Silberstein's admirers, his son-in-law Burton Slatkin, Muriel's husband, seems to resent comparisons between his father-in-law and Courtright. The difference between the two, he says, is that Silberstein is a direct, firm man. If he doesn't like something, he will let you know, immediately and with no subterfuge.

But Courtright, "he's sweet to your face" and then zings you with a tart memo, Slatkin says.

It didn't take long before the dalliance between Mr. S.

The sign of an institution. *(Gernot Kuehn)*

The Beverly Hills soon after it opened. That rutty road in the foreground is now the heavily trafficked Sunset Boulevard. *(Los Angeles Public Library)*

The hotel looking less forlorn a few years later. To the left is the old Toonerville trolley that carried guests and servants from the train station to the hotel. *(Los Angeles Public Library)*

A room service waiter wheels the remains of a lunch through the garden.
(Gernot Kuehn)

A Beverly Hills bungalow. *(Gernot Kuehn)*

Comedian Marty Allen sometimes breaks into his Las Vegas routine at the front desk. *(Ron Galella)*

Barbara Stanwyck gets greeted by the Easter bunny under the porte-cochere. *(Ron Galella)*

Gregory Peck, as president of the Academy of Motion Picture Arts and Scienc held an Oscars press conference at the hotel pool in 1968. He's sitting on the diving board. *(Ron Galella)*

The gentleman with Elizabeth Taylor is diet doctor Lou Scarone. The two had just talked over something weighty in the Polo Lounge. *(Ron Galella)*

Ted Kennedy and niece Courtney attending a benefit for former California Senator John Tunney at the hotel. Brothers Bobby and Jack used the Beverly Hills as a favored trysting spot. *(Ron Galella)*

One of Charlie's angels, Jaclyn Smith. *(Ron Galel*

No Rolls or Mercedes for Doris Day and husband Barry. They arrived on bicycle for breakfast in the coffee shop. Here they unsuccessfully try to avoid photographe by leaving Doris' bike parked at the porte-cochere and taking a side exit. *(Ron Galella)*

Swooping off Sunset Boulevard up to the Beverly Hills. *(Gernot Kuehn)*

Cher making an entrance. In the 1950s she wouldn't have been allowed into the Polo Lounge in that outfit. Women in pants had to wear a pink wrap-around skirt for the sake of propriety. *(Ron Galella)*

It was a happy Halston in March, 1976, but he wasn't smiling the first time he came to the hotel. The designer was almost thrown out when he wouldn't sign his full name on the registry. *(Ron Galella)*

David Frost has a policy of never tipping anyone — but he gets his car anyway.
(Ron Galella)

Liza Minnelli at the front desk, 1970. She and her two cats took refuge at the hotel while her house was being painted (Ron Galella)

Jack Webb waits outside the Polo Lounge near the elevator. (Ron Galella)

Debbie Reynolds and Cesar Romero on their way to a fashion show.
The two stopped to smile in the lower level arcade. *(Ron Galella)*

Lucille Ball strutting her stuff at a benefit fashion show in 1968. *(Ron Galella)*

Singer Linda Ronstadt. *(Ron Galella)*

Broadway producer David Merrick.
(Ron Galella)

t's CBS's Mike Wallace munching on
apple as his car is being fetched.
n Galella)

Zsa Zsa Gabor on the red carpet.
(Ron Galella)

Jack Nicholson waits for his car, tip in hand. The woman with him is Angelica Huston. *(Ron Galella)*

and Courtright's missus was the whisper of the hotel. Even if liaisons between the two hadn't been noticed—which would have been hard, since secrets can't be kept for long in a hotel—the friction between the men became increasingly apparent. Communication ceased. Pettiness began. Silberstein would order a potted palm moved to *this* corner of the lobby. Courtright would spot it the next morning and order it moved to *that* corner.

Divorce was inevitable.

When it was final, Rosalind married Silberstein.

The Los Angeles Times reported, August 27, 1958:

> *Hernando Courtright, colorful hotel figure, who has personally controlled and managed the Beverly Hills Hotel for 22 years, announced yesterday that he has resigned as president and director of the hostelry with the completion of a transaction in which the hotel was acquired by Benjamin Silberstein and associates, of Detroit. . . .*
>
> *Courtright said he had made no decisions or commitments as to his future activities.*

Silberstein made final payment on the hotel six months early. It was now his. A Detroit newspaper account said that Courtright had agreed to retire on receipt of the final payment.

There was no mention of Rosalind.

The animosity between Courtright and Silberstein did not abate.

Courtright feigns forgetting "Silverberg's" name; Silberstein is an amnesiac when it comes to Courtright.

People had said that Silberstein was no hotelman, that anyone with a modicum of business sense could have made a go of the Beverly Hills after Courtright had established it. But the hotel was Silberstein's, his palace, and Courtright had been deposed. Silberstein had taken the queen and the castle. He had won the game. Checkmate.

Now it may be that Silberstein wasn't a hotelman. But he had enough sense and enough feeling for what he had purchased to leave it be. He could have gone for the fast buck, skimped a little here, gouged a little there, but he chose instead to maintain the standards of the hotel and use his money to raise them higher.

Slatkin maintains that Courtright, in his reign, made flashy, visible changes in the hotel. Silberstein did solid things that didn't show, improvements that desperately needed to be made. The new plumbing. Air conditioning. Bungalows razed and completely rebuilt.

If Silberstein had let standards at the Beverly Hills slip, chances are Hernando Courtright would have won their rematch, for he didn't go limping off to lick his wounded pride, never to be seen again. On the contrary, when given the chance to take on Silberstein again, he seized it.

After leaving the Beverly Hills, Courtright hooked up with William Zeckendorf in a little project known as Century City. They envisioned a "Rockefeller Center West" of office buildings, stores, theaters, and restaurants to jut up like the Emerald City on a plot of land that had been the back lot of 20th Century-Fox. It was a splendid idea, and one that would eventually be realized, but unfortunately Zeckendorf and Courtright didn't have the bankroll of Rockefeller. They ran out of money before the project was completed. Century City, with its Avenue of the Stars and Gelson's—the best food store west of the Pennington Market in New Jersey—was eventually completed by Alcoa.

Courtright being Courtright, the loss of the Century City project didn't leave him on a short road to nowhere. It only meant he would have to find something new.

As mentioned earlier, William Zeckendorf was one of the fifteen or twenty "guys who buy properties." The guys are usually into more than one deal at a time. Buy a parking lot here. Unload an apartment house there. That kind of thing.

In 1955 in one of these fast shuffles, Webb and Knapp, the corporation Zeckendorf was with, ended up with the Gotham Hotel in New York and the Beverly Wilshire in California. (It also bought the lease to the Nacional in

Cuba, a hotel owned by the Cuban government. Luckily for Webb and Knapp, they sold the lease to the Corporacion Intercontinental de Hoteles de Cuba, reportedly a subsidiary of Pan American World Airways, before Dr. Fidel Castro and his barbudos marched into Havana and the lease became worth the paper it was printed on.)

The Beverly Wilshire, while never falling into bankruptcy, had fallen onto hard times. As writer Stephen Birmingham put it, "It had become a hotel for conventioneers and itinerant drummers." Seedy, dilapidated, dreary. Webb and Knapp was more than happy to sell it to Courtright, who again got a little help from his friends, although this time he was to be the principal stockholder.

Again they were nice friends, friends like realtor Roger Stevens; Jimmy Stewart; Irene Dunne; former head of Magnavox Richard O'Connor; Gregory Peck; Kirk Douglas; Earle Jorgensen, a big man in the steel industry; Henry Salvatori, a big man in the oil industry; Nils Onstad, a big man in Swedish industry and also Sonja Henie's husband; Edward Carter of the Broadway-Hale chain; Harry Volk of Union Bank; and the Walt Disney estate.

His dislike for Silberstein must have inspired him. Courtright set out to transform the Beverly Wilshire into a showcase that would outsplendor everything in Southern California.

The renaissance took place on a grand and costly scale. Not only would he redo the pseudo-Florentine palazzo (the first order of business was removing a garish neon sign from the roof), but he would build a 250-room, ten-story tower behind it, with a new "street' between the wings to make arriving by car easier. (Unloading and loading at the old entrance on busy Wilshire Boulevard had become a harrowing and inelegant business.) The new tower, with interior decorations, ran seven million dollars over budget.

Final cost: twenty-two million dollars.

One reason for the overrun was the care taken in decorating by Courtright's new wife, a beautiful Mexican named Marcelle.

She was a perfectionist. She searched out perfect pear trees to line the entrance of the new street. She brought stonecutters over from Italy to shape the granite blocks for the driveway. She bought wall hangings from one tribe of Mexican Indians and handmade boxes from another. (The only way to reach the second tribe was by helicopter.) Walls weren't painted; they were covered with French fabric. The drapes used in one room were patterned after a hanging in the Metropolitan Museum in New York. The museum was paid royalties for use of the design.

A friend was to explain, "If there was one thing Hernando loved more than his hotel it was Marcelle. He gave her complete freedom in terms of decor, and she went at it as though the sky were the limit."

The result is startling, a lovely hotel serviced with the same graciousness that Courtright instilled in the Beverly Hills.

(Tragically, Marcelle, though many years younger than Courtright, died before the hotel was finished. During her illness Courtright started drinking cranberry juice instead of wine. He explained to a friend that the juice's acid was good for the kidneys. Later he confessed, "I wasn't telling you the truth about the cranberry juice. There's nothing the matter with my kidneys, and you know how much I love my wine. But the other day I decided to give up wine—for Marcelle. I said to God, I'll give up everything I love the most, if you'll just let me keep Marcelle.")

§   §   §   §   §   §   §   §   §   §

Meanwhile back at the Beverly Hills, Silberstein was having family problems, some of which probably delighted Courtright.

First there was Silberstein's sister Mrs. Hattie S. Sloan,

whom he hadn't spoken to for years. In 1959, as reported by the *Detroit Free Press*, she renewed contact by suing her brother for allegedly mishandling their mother's trust fund.

Mother Mary had died in March 1941. Her estate was then worth $614,530 in personal property and real estate. Silberstein was named one of the trustees. According to sister Hattie, Ben used his position to secure a loan for $71,274, using the mortgage on one of the trust properties as security. Some of the loan money was actually used to make improvements on the trust property. But, charged sister, the rest was improperly used to acquire twenty-five thousand shares in the First National Bank Building. By law, any profits derived from a trust fund are supposed to go back to the fund. Not so in this case, Hattie said. Furthermore she charged that at about the same time Ben was negotiating purchase of the Beverly Hills, he had relocated all the trust's cash into the account of the Silberstein Realty Company. This "loan," he then repaid without interest.

"The co-mingling of funds of the Silberstein Realty Company with the trust fund is not conducive to proper management of the trust estate and is not in the best interest of the beneficiaries," Hattie's suit claimed.

In February 1965, the *Free Press* reported that the court had sided with sister Hattie.

Silberstein, said the story, "accused of mismanaging a million-dollar trust fund was ordered Friday to repay $737,000 to the trust.

"Circuit Judge Joseph A. Sullivan ordered Ben Silberstein, now of Palm Beach, Fla., to make the repayment to the estate of Silberstein's mother, Mrs. Mary Silberstein."

A year later the State of Michigan Appeals Court reduced the award to $109,990.95. Of course, Hattie did not receive that full sum. She had only a fifth interest in the trust, as did Ben. Further, according to Slatkin, "all of Hattie's charges of trust mismanagement, co-mingling of funds, etc., etc., were dismissed. The amount awarded was a compromise, and was essentially a vindication of Ben's actions and position."

§   §   §   §   §   §   §   §   §   §

And then there was Rosalind. The marriage was a bust. Some cynics suggested the spark had gone out of the romance at the moment Courtright made his exit. Be that as it may, the marriage was on the rocks. Unfortunately for Silberstein it was on the rocks in California, the land of fifty-fifty community-property settlement.

It was about this time that Silberstein opted for Florida's sunshine instead of California's.

It was there that Cupid torpedoed Ben L. Silberstein again. It was there that he met Bonnie Edwards, a beautiful ex Broadway dancer. Among her several previous husbands was Tommy Manville, but it was a divorce settlement from Charles Wilson, a wealthy Britisher, that allowed her to become part of the poshy Palm Beach society, a society established by Marjorie Merriweather Post when she realized the Blue Book would be closed on her in Boston, New York, and Philadelphia.

Once Rosalind was an "ex," Silberstein made Bonnie his current, which she is still.

Some fifteen or twenty years younger than Silberstein, Bonnie is one of those women Age has overlooked. She is unflappably cool, her composure resolute.

Witness the day Silberstein flared up at her in the lobby. She stood calmly as he railed at her. She did nothing when suddenly he slapped her. Nothing except wordlessly take out a handkerchief and dab away the blood.

Not that Bonnie has never been ready to cash in her chips. On one occasion she had packed her bags and was on the way out, when Slatkin intercepted her. Reasoned with her. Talked her into staying.

(Some of the longtime switchboard operators say that in

the prenuptial agreement, Bonnie relinquished all claims on Silberstein's estate, but her daughters will receive a trust.)

If Silberstein had been looking for nothing but a woman to project a good image for the hotel, he couldn't have done better than Bonnie. She is *Town and Country* beige and cordial, someone easily able to make a gracious impression.

In the past, the two pretty much led their own lives. She traveled a lot, and alone, and he has the Room That Doesn't Exist, Room 100, which the desk clerks are not supposed to book, in case Mr. S. or his friends should want it for privacy.

Silberstein is now in his mid-seventies and remains irascible and temperamental on how things will be in his domain. A 1976 article in *New West* magazine, although primarily favorable, infuriated him with a vignette between the writer Jon Bradshaw and a part-time hooker he encountered in the Polo Lounge.

Silberstein ruled that the Beverly Hills Hotel needed no further publicity and would cooperate with writers no longer. It is one of the few hotels in the world that probably won't be harmed if stories are not written about it. It has a reputation that transcends publicity.

(The hotel has been approached in the past by authors—including Gore Vidal and Joyce Haber—who wanted to do a book on the Beverly Hills. But always in the past, management refused to cooperate. It deigned to talk at all for this book only when it recognized that it is one thing to stonewall a possible book and quite another to be faced with the reality of an existing one.)

In any case, Silberstein still wields the stick, although it is his son-in-law, Slatkin, president of the hotel, who runs the show now.

Muriel never lost the attraction she felt for the Beverly Hills at eighteen. She's made it her life.

The hotel is her demesne, as it is her father's domaine.

She's very much a social creature, with the looks of a Kitty Carlisle, giving teas and luncheons; raising money for cancer research; getting mentioned in the *Los Angeles Times* society columns; hanging around with Grace Robbins, writer Harold Robbins's wife, the Sammy Cahns, and Christina Onassis when she's in town; arranging the employees' Christmas party. (One grinchy employee grumbled he'd rather skip this party if attending meant taking part in arrangement meetings without pay.)

She and Slatkin live in a *House Beautiful* home behind the hotel, but she is in and out of the hotel constantly. She grew up there; it's hers. Her friends find her delightful, but some of the employees chafe under her reign, complaining that her attitude is too imperial.

"Her appearance at those Christmas parties," says one former employee, "is like a once-a-year visit from the queen."

But then again, it is hers. And if she wants to rearrange the window in the drugstore—a $250,000-a-year enterprise that is not a concession, as most of the other shops are, but is owned by the hotel—so be it. Her father, after all, has a couch in the lobby that he insists must be in a certain spot. He even has a mark on the wall to double-check that it is.

There is one story of Muriel's strong-willed proprietorship that began with a Beverly Hills cop ticketing her not far from the hotel.

It was the habit of the police patrolling the area to drop into the hotel and have coffee in the front office. A couple of days after the ticketing that very cop was having coffee there, when Muriel spotted him. Out, she ordered, and furthermore, out to all the cops. *No more free coffee at the Beverly Hills Hotel.*

No more free coffee! It was a perk the cops would fight for. War was declared. The cops started a ticketing blitz. Any infraction, no matter how small, committed in the vicinity of the Beverly Hills Hotel got slapped with a fine.

Even the two-hour parking laws on the side streets, which no one pays attention to, were suddenly being enforced.

It took about a month before things were back to normal, enough time for all sides to save face and for the cops to be back in the front office slurping caffeine.

That's how the story goes, although her husband maintains that "certain new police officers who became overzealous in suddenly enforcing certain parking laws on side streets adjacent to the Hotel were told by our Manager to seek their coffee breaks elsewhere. This problem was quickly resolved to the satisfaction of everyone."

Slatkin, an affable man, is always on the verge of getting fat. One symptom is his lust for the hotel's petit fours.

"If you're looking for Slatkin," someone once said, "check the pastry corner in the kitchen first."

Unfortunately, his wife does a Sherlock Holmes and is on to this particular weakness, occasionally filling his soul with guilt as he fills his stomach with hard candy.

Raiding the kitchen is a fringe benefit of a family business, Slatkin says.

He has been president for the past five years, but his father-in-law, who lives in the hotel, has not relinquished all control.

"If there is something wrong, he lets me know. The more eyes to observe, the better." Slatkin's two sons, one of whom now works in a motel chain the Beverly Hills corporation bought into a few years ago, and the other of whom took one year at the Cornell School of Hotel Management before transferring to liberal arts ("Other students were being introduced to philosophy while he was learning how to make an omelet"), are also on the alert for ways to improve the operation. Slatkin expects the hotel to remain in the family through the next generation.

"This hotel is a personalized ego thing for us," he explains.

Silberstein's other daughter, Seema, now Mrs. Seema Boetsky of New York, is not involved with the hotel. When her children were younger she came to visit one year, bringing along a fleet of bicycles that were strewn outside her bungalow, causing other guests to complain. The complainers were told to go to another hotel if they didn't like bikes.

Muriel and Seema's mother, who married a Detroit doctor, would also visit once a year. Thanks to Muriel's intervention, things were more cordial after the divorce.

It's going on twenty-five years since that real estate investor from Detroit went *click, click, bing,* and dollar signs flashed before his eyes. In that time he's maintained an institution, overseen a realm, and been part of a fantasy world that, no matter how mundane it might be on any given day, was indeed a Pink Palace.

It may seem fanciful to believe that some stucco and tile could capture and entrance such different people as Mrs. Margaret Anderson, Hernando Courtright, and Ben L. Silberstein.

But somehow it did.

Part Two

Chapter Seven

The man in the short white jacket was very good at his job.

He carefully checked the Sterno burner. Too high a temperature, and the food would dry out; too low, and it would be cool. After years of checking Sterno burners, the man knew the perfect temperature.

He laid out the silver (first looking for remnants of someone else's meal) in traditional, formal setting. He poured water into the water goblet, without a drop dripped. Rolls were felt for warmness and then re-covered with a pink cloth napkin. He placed the one perfect red rose in its slender ceramic vase to the side, to be admired without being obtrusive.

Out came a warmed plate from beneath the serving cart. And then the man in the short white jacket spooned and arranged the entrée so it rivaled the most appetizing, glossy centerfold in *Gourmet*.

With all this done, Bernie Bloch, the peerless head of room service, shook out a second pink napkin and held it out for the man he was serving. The guest's broad, jowly, and invariably grim face had been made familiar by countless exposures on the nightly network news and on the front pages of the nation's newspapers. It was the face of one of the President's Men, one of Richard Milhous Nixon's closest advisers.

It was the face of John Mitchell.

Mitchell had been attorney general of the United States, but now he was Nixon's campaign manager, director of the Committee for the Re-election of the President (CREEP).

Bloch figured Mitchell was in town to raise more money for the party coffers. There had been other Nixon big guns floating around the hotel lobby, H. R. Haldeman among them. Bloch would have recognized these men without any coaching from Walter Cronkite. They were hundred-dollar tippers—which was why, as head of room service, Bloch always waited on John Mitchell.

The television had been on and was humming the news. As he worked, Bloch had caught a snatch or two.

George McGovern expected to win most of the New York delegates.

Heavy bombing in North Vietnam.

Fiddler on the Roof *becomes the longest-running show on Broadway.*

There was another item, one that Bloch would have assuredly dismissed as trivial and inconsequential someone living three thousand miles from it in Southern California.

It seems that something called the Watergate had been broken into by five men. More specifically, the offices of the Democratic National Committee, which were in the Watergate, had been burglarized.

"Junkies or crazy Cubans" is probably how Bloch would have dismissed the item—except for John Mitchell's reaction to it.

"Son of a bitch!" Mitchell suddenly yelled. "Goddamn! They blew it! They blew it!"

Mitchell was overwrought. He pushed the table back and stopped yelling at the television long enough to yell at Bloch, "Take the food away. Take everything away. I've got to get to the telephone. Out of the room!"

That was June 17, 1972. On June 18, Mitchell announced

to anyone who cared to listen that the burglars at Watergate "were not operating on either our behalf or with our consent. There is no place in our campaign or in the electoral process for this type of activity, and we will not permit or condone it."

Bernie Bloch knew better. So did the other staff members he told of the incident.

The rest of the world had to wait for Woodward and Bernstein to sort out the Watergate mess. But the staff at the Beverly Hills Hotel knew Mitchell was involved from the beginning.

§   §   §   §   §   §   §   §   §   §

The staff knows everything. Everything of interest. The employees of a hotel may be a faceless blur to most guests who twirl in and out, tending to business or pleasure, using the hotel as a background to what they are doing.

But a hotel is a good portion of the staff's life. Those on the payroll are there day after day, week after week, and in the case of the Beverly Hills, year after year. They are part of a close and intimate world, a community in which secrets are hard to keep.

It's not just that the staff is charged to notice what is happening. What is happening makes their existence more interesting. It gives them something to talk about.

"Did you see David Niven in tears at the front desk when he couldn't get the room he wanted?"

"Did you hear the latest about Lauren Bacall? She screamed that the maids had switched the top sheet with the bottom instead of putting clean ones on the bed."

What is happening at the Beverly Hills gives the staff an intimacy with the beautiful, rich, noteworthy, and powerful, the greats and those trying hard to be great. Working at the Beverly Hills affords an insider's status. It makes you privy to the secrets and souls of special people.

Sometimes it lets the employees know things the rest of the country is wondering about.

§   §   §   §   §   §   §   §   §   §

Diamond Liz Taylor was rockless when she sang on the Academy Award show in 1975.

Liz, separated from Richard Burton at the time, was hanging out with ex used-car salesman Henry Wynberg. Her jewels, however, were tucked away in a safe-deposit box at the Beverly Hills Hotel.

Ordinarily, when a guest rents a box at the hotel, the guest is given the key. But Liz was nervous about carrying one through the wilds of Truesdale (a most expensive place to have an address) and tried to get someone in the front office to guard it.

No soap. If any little bauble should happen to turn up missing later—and with Taylor's lackadaisical handling of her jewels, that wasn't out of the question—the guardian of the key would be held responsible.

Finally Taylor was able to prevail upon her new manager to hold the key to her safe-deposit box. He thought it was kind of exciting, it being Liz Taylor's key and all.

All well and good until she arrived to collect some of her rocks to wear at the Oscar presentations. All well and good except that manager was out playing golf—gone for day, and no one knew at which course. There was nothing to be done.

Diamond Liz had to go rockless.

§   §   §   §   §   §   §   §   §   §

At the Maumee Holiday Inn, a late-night call from a drunk Mr. Whoever demanding to speak to his wife might make the graveyard shift pass a little faster. But the same call from a Someone, a Star, a Nielsen Numbers Grabber, a

Box-office Champ, that is something worth talking about.

§   §   §   §   §   §   §   §   §   §

It's about the time when all good wives and husbands should be in bed—with each other—when a call comes through to the front desk.

"This is Steve McQueen," said Steve McQueen, sounding sloshy enough for the clerk to think, *Oh, Jesus, drunk again.*

"I want to talk to my wife. I know she is there with Warren Beatty."

The clerk assured McQueen that Ali McGraw had not been seen all evening, adding, "If she is with Mr. Beatty, I would suggest you try the Wilshire. He has a suite there, you know, not here."

McQueen, doing a Duke Mantee, growled, "Listen, you, check the Polo Lounge. Ali always goes to the Beverly Hills."

Polo Lounge, check.

"I am sorry, sir, she is not there, and she is not here."

McQueen knew better, he insisted. When Ali messes around, he said, she messes around at the Beverly Hills. That had been her spot with McQueen when they had slipped around on her then husband, Bob Evans. It must be her spot with Beatty.

The staff at the Beverly Hills *knew* that marriage wouldn't last.

§   §   §   §   §   §   §   §   §   §

It's easier for the staff to know all at the Beverly Hills because of the Beverly Hills Treatment—its extraordinary vintaged style of service; its catering to and care of guests; its little extras that make it a wonderful hotel.

The hotel knows which extras are preferred by which

guests (some like a bottle of Scotch; others a bouquet of carnations) by a card file it keeps on likes and dislikes.

Any good *So You Want to Be a Hotel Manager* textbook directs the novice to keep such a card file, but the trick and the difference between the Beverly Hills and the Lennox Hotel in "revitalized downtown" Saint Louis is the extent and types of notations made on the card.

The Beverly Hills knows not only which room a guest prefers, but the niceties down to the smallest touches that have pleased a guest in the past.

Some notations are common sense. Just as an RCA TV was carted into 486 for General Sarnoff, Gillette executives find Gillette blades in their bathroom cabinets.

In his room bar, Commander Whitehead always found bottles of Schweppes, naturally, and a bottle of gin. Not any gin, mind you. Commander Whitehead had a preference for Beefeater's. He also liked to take early-morning swims. The pool opens at 10, but the commander liked to get his laps in closer to the crack of dawn. His athletic proclivities were noted on his card with a reminder that he should be automatically be given a key to the pool gate on his arrival.

This card system allows more common folk to get treatment similar to what was afforded Lord Snowdon and Princess Margaret on their first visit together.

It was 1965. The staff was extensively instructed how to mind their protocol and punctilios. The royal couple must be addressed as ma'am and sir, the British consulate had advised. Maids and waiters and bellmen were never to speak unless spoken to, to keep a minimum of five feet away from the lord and his princess, and to keep heads bowed when receiving an order.

The staff was further advised that their highnesses would ordinarily leave through the lobby—imagine all those craning heads trying to get a peek at them—but Tony and Meg might be slipping out to a discotheque through the garage.

Stewart Hathaway, the manager then, wasn't worried

that his staff couldn't handle the assignment. It had lots of practice. Besides, he said, although Princess Margaret was a stickler for certain formalities, "our charm is friendliness, not stiffness. I think our staff is a little like me, a bit of a ham, and that is good."

In keeping with that friendliness when it was discovered that Lord Snowdon smoked Gauloises, a French cigarette unavailable in the boondocks of Los Angeles, the hotel had a few cartons flown in for his enjoyment. And it made sure that the princess got her gin and tonic—she didn't like champagne—and that he got his Scotch. Management even took pains to find out what they liked for breakfast. So without asking the princess got her fresh fruit and rolls, and her husband his eggs and ham, bacon, or sausage— and of course, tea, but tea always made with distilled water.

Suite 486 had been completely redecorated before their arrival. One of the last things brought in was a large expensive mirror—which cracked as it was being installed.

Frantic searching and activity consumed the entire night before a replacement mirror was installed before Princess Margaret made her appearance.

Royal treatment at the Beverly Hills is not reserved only for descendants of Elizabeth I. In little ways, in larger ways, the hotel strives to coddle and delight its visitors.

Robert Mitchum, as noted on his guest card, was to be served the taste-boggling concoction of bourbon in orange juice mixed with eggs and honey.

Van Johnson wants only red napkins.

Fresh flowers are never placed on the tray of an unnamed lady—their wilting depresses her.

Phyllis Diller fancies that Turkish delight *shaslik*.

Laurence Harvey craved the heels of French bread. (His card was flagged to alert the cook to save them.)

Elizabeth Taylor freaked for potatoes smothered in sour cream and caviar à la Maxim's in Paris. (The hotel finally put that dish on the Coterie Restaurant menu.)

Another of Elizabeth's noted yens is pistachio nuts,

which are thoughtfully put into her room so that she may start munching two steps over the threshold.

During her Burton period, a fresh bucket of ice went automatically to her bungalow on the hour.

Over the years the lady's card has become a small encyclopedia as her tastes and appetites have changed.

Of course, in the case of Elizabeth, there has been some amused consternation over her habit of changing her preferred bungalow when she changed husbands. Having stayed in bungalow 3 with Fisher, she moved to 8 with Burton. Would the hotel run out of bungalows before Elizabeth ran out of husbands?

Some of the lengths the hotel has gone to for guests have become near legends.

The Texas oil man and the bear steak.

It has been told that a very wealthy oil man (no name is ever mentioned) once ordered broiled bear steak for dinner.

Now at most any other hotel, such a request would get a "Sorry; it's not on the menu." But the Beverly Hills prides itself in going to extraordinary lengths to provide what a guest wants.

However, finding a bear steak in Los Angeles proved quite impossible—it's not, after all, a standard shelf item at Ralphs Supermarket.

The hotel was chagrined. Its reputation at stake. Amends had to be made. The next time the oil man reserved a room, the hotel, as legend has it, had frozen bear steaks flown in.

It's a great legend. Almost true.

What actually happened began as a gag, a long-running gag.

There was a Texas oil millionaire, and he did take delight in asking Ruth Pokorney, the lady at the other end of the room-service line, the same question every time he was at the hotel.

"You got any bear steaks, honey?"

You got any bear steaks, honey? Why would the hotel

even want to have bear steaks? Eventually the little joke would have got to anyone, but Ruth Pokorney had been John Barrymore's secretary for three years. And Barrymore was never one to tolerate jokers, Texas millionaires or otherwise.

In early 1962, Ruth got revenge.

She had heard through the active hotel grapevine that the Texan was due to arrive. Ever so sweetly, she informed manager Hathaway of the millionaire's repeated inquiry. What Hathaway thought of the request is not known, but it was known that he was anxious to give his guests precisely what they wanted.

Consequently, frozen bear steaks were indeed flown in from Alaska.

With the next "You got any bear steaks, honey?" Ruth was able to answer gleefully, "Yes. Would you like them rare, medium, or well done?"

There wasn't much the Texas millionaire could do.

He ate the bear steaks.

His reaction to the meal is unknown.

§   §   §   §   §   §   §   §   §   §

Not that that has been the only out-of-the-ordinary, hard-to-satisfy request ever granted at the hotel.

One Prince Khaiber Khan wanted cous-cous for a banquet he was giving. In the land of salad bars and barbeques, cous-cous was not your everyday dish, and the hotel's banquet chef, Garry Reich, didn't have the slightest notion what it was. However, when a guest of the hotel, particularly a prince, wants cous-cous, then cous-cous he gets.

An admirable attitude, except that none of the cookbooks in Reich's library even mentioned the dish, much less gave a recipe for it.

Undaunted, he called every cook and food fancier he knew, seeking a clue. No luck, until he uncovered a tiny Middle Eastern restaurant, The Fez, in Hollywood. The chef there was delighted to supply his more esteemed counterpart with directions for his culinary secret.

On schedule, as requested, the prince got his couscous—a delectably broiled mixture of mutton, cabbage squash, and carrots, all plopped on a thick bed of farina.

§   §   §   §   §   §   §   §   §   §

As might be expected, some guests get treated to more of the Beverly Hills Treatment than others. Everyone might be "royalty," but there are queens and kings, and then there are barons and dukes, down to knights who had the sword tapped on the shoulders only last week. That's life even in a Pink Palace—or perhaps especially in a Pink Palace.

To keep track of this hierarchy, the hotel has a color-coded cross-reference in the card file. Some cards are white, some blue, a very, very few are pink (what else?).

The Beverly Hills can be choosy about its guests. First off, 75 percent of them have been to the hotel before. Second off, the hotel has as close to 100-percent occupancy as it can get—in fact, it often has 110-percent occupancy. The hotel has sometimes overbooked as many as thirty or forty a night. (Overbooked guests are placed at other hotels, a practice called farming. A sign once hung in the office behind the front desk, NEVER FARM TO THE BEVERLY WILSHIRE.)

§   §   §   §   §   §   §   §   §   §

It was early evening. A high-echelon executive, a Revlon lady, was attempting to register. It was her first stay at the hotel.

"I'm terribly sorry, madam," the desk clerk was saying, "but unfortunately, we don't have a room for you here tonight."

"I don't understand," the woman said, pulling out an

envelope. "Right here is a written confirmation of my reservation. This *is* the Beverly Hills Hotel, isn't it?"

Yes, it is, madam, and we deeply regret this inconvenience. But there is no room. We will, however, get you a very nice accommodation at another hotel. There's the Century Plaza, the Beverly Hilton, perhaps even the Bel-Air. . . .

The woman interrupted. "If I wanted to go to the Century Plaza, Beverly Hilton, or Bel-Air, I would have made a reservation at the Century Plaza, Beverly Hilton, or Bel-Air. I wanted to come here. That's why I had my secretary call you and why she got a written confirmation. Now, I don't understand why there is no room for me."

Heads were turning. A scene was being created. The clerk fetched the assistant night manager, Ernie Brown, a courteous man who for obvious reasons always played Santa Claus at the employee Christmas party. After more than twenty years at the hotel, Brown was a consummate smoother of ruffled feathers. He escorted the Revlon lady to a chair, out of the lobby flow.

Offering more apologies, Brown assured the lady that as soon as a room was available, the Beverly Hills would have her luggage transported back. . . . Once in a while, a problem such as this arises . . . hopes she understands . . . terribly sorry . . . and so on. It wasn't the first time Brown had played this scene.

The woman was having none of it. Patiently, calmly, she said, "At this point, I don't particularly want to stay at the Beverly Hills Hotel. I'm sure these other hotels are quite adequate. However, I have a very busy appointment schedule set up out here. I have a lot to accomplish, and all the people I'm going to see have been told I'm staying here. They have this number. My suddenly going to another hotel will make it difficult for some of these people to contact me. Which might mean my schedule will be thrown off and I won't get things done. So you see, I must stay here."

The woman was remaining completely reasonable even as Brown again began to state his regrets.

"All right," the lady interrupted. "I will sleep over there on that couch." She pointed to one placed before the ever-burning hearth of friendliness and hospitality. She picked up her bag, carried it to the couch, and removed a negligee.

Brown, and almost everyone else in the lobby, stood transfixed. It wasn't possible, and yet the woman was undressing. One button, two, three, four . . . The lady wasn't bluffing. Five buttons, six . . . She managed to get her blouse open and was going for the hooks on her bra, when Brown was snapped from his trance.

This was an emergency. Brown suddenly remembered a vacant suite the woman could have that night for the price of a room. Her things would be moved to a room once one became available.

Anything to get her out of the lobby!

§ § § § § § § § § §

The lady was a white card.

Most first timers who aren't Lord Snowdon and Princess Margaret are.

White cards are the lowest rank of the Pink Palace nobility. When there is overbooking, they get farmed first. Within the white cards there exists a subranking. Newlyweds are only slightly better than commoners, commoners being those misbegotten riff-raff who can't even get a reservation. Newlyweds can, but they often end up elsewhere. They are usually couples who get married in Los Angeles and start their honeymoon trip with a one-night stay at a hotel in town before going on to Hawaii or Acapulco. If they choose the Beverly Hills, and if they are unlucky enough to get there on an overbooked night, they are the first to be farmed. The rationale is that in all likelihood, it would be quite some time before the couple can afford a return visit.

Samuel Bronfman II, heir to the Seagram's fortune, got farmed out on his wedding night. Even the notoriety of his kidnapping the year before could not get him a room.

Most guests of the hotel are blue cards. On these cards are listed when you've been there before, how long you've stayed, which room you stayed in, any complaints, any special requests you might have had. Naturally, after a time, the information on the card becomes more extensive.

Silberstein once called the cards a gimmick but a nice gimmick, nice to be greeted with, "Ms. Smith, so nice to see you again. It's been seven months now, hasn't it? We've put you back into Room 375, since you enjoyed it so much last time."

You're not anonymous at the Beverly Hills. You've come home to where they seem to appreciate having you, look forward to having you. Where when you reach your room after check-in, pick up your phone to make a call, the switchboard operator says, "Yes, Ms. Jones? What number would you like?"

Then there are the pink cards.

Pink cards are the Very Special Treatment people, the ones who no effort is too great to please, kings and queens and emperors visiting the Pink Palace, personages to be treated with pomp, ceremony, friendliness, and care.

It's not easy getting onto a pink card. In fact, it's next to impossible. The Fords—of Grosse Pointe, not Grand Rapids—are pink cards. Arab kings and princes are pink cards, as are some Arab businessmen, especially if they are Adnan Khashoggi. Onassis was a pink card. He always tipped 25 percent.

The very top movie stars are pink cards, but not all the top television stars.

The big guests booked on the *Tonight* show are pink cards, but only because they are carte blanched by the NBC accounting office.

Famous people, rich people, powerful people are pink cards, although being famous, rich, or powerful doesn't guarantee a pink card. You must be famous by the Beverly Hills' standards, by its ken and knowledge, powerful to the Beverly Hills' perception and liking, and rich. The rich have a good shot at a pink card as long as they behave themselves and tip the right people generously.

Lyndon Baines Johnson used to stay at the Beverly Hills. He and Lady Bird initially were white cards. After a time he was elevated to a blue card—primarily, it was said, because of her family and money, rather than his ascendancy in Washington.

When Johnson became vice-president of the United States, his new job was duly noted next to the space for "occupation" on his blue card. After John F. Kennedy's assassination, his new job was also duly noted. The "vice" was crossed off, but Johnson was never elevated to a pink card.

The Beverly Hills is not partial to politicians. The Kennedys were welcomed despite their governmental attachments. When the Democratic nominating convention was held in Los Angeles in 1960, delegates were not welcomed at the Beverly Hills.

Said a spokesman, "We did not allot any space to the convention bureau. We wanted to save it all for our old and dear friends."

Among those "old and dear friends" were Adlai Stevenson's sons, Stuart Symington's family, and Perle Mesta.

Politicians, like conventioneers, bring too much hurly-burly along with their baggage. It doesn't add to the hotel's image or operation to have Secret Service men lurking behind potted plants.

Once upon a time, press people were automatic pink cards. Although undoubtedly an unsavory lot, they were pandered to for their influence. Bad publicity was to be avoided at all costs. (Muriel was overheard complaining, "Rex Reed is a faggot, and I hate him. But what can I do? He's a writer.")

Sometimes the perception at the Beverly Hills of who is

important is very different from the rest of the world's.

§ § § § § § § § § §

Halston was a name with clout in New York. Readers of both *Womens Wear Daily* and the *Daily News* knew who Halston was. Why, he was the designing darling of Jackie Oh! Liza Minnelli, Bianca Jagger, and other ultrachics who didn't faint at his price tags.

But Halston wasn't in New York. He was in Beverly Hills escorting Marisa Berenson to the Academy Awards ceremonies. Marisa needed a "walker," being temporarily manless. Her romance with Ricky Von Opel, of the European automobile family, had fizzled. It was Halston to the rescue.

He and his male traveling companion, an Argentinian named Victor Hugo, had arrived at the front desk of the Beverly Hills Hotel, and to Halston's indignation the desk clerk was asking him to supply his first *and* last names.

"What are you talking about?" Halston sputtered. "I am Halston."

"Of course, sir," the clerk said, "but I must have your entire name."

'Halston! I am *Halston!* That's all! My picture has been in *Time* magazine.

Unimpressed—guests of the hotel often have their pictures in *Time* magazine — the clerk again explained that unless Mr. Halston was prepared to follow hotel rules, the hotel was not prepared to give *Mr.* Halston a room.

After hemming, hawing, and face-saving, Hugo capitulated, signing in first and last names for them both. Only then were they given a room.

§ § § § § § § § § §

Had Halston refused to sign, he would have been turned

away, and the hotel would not have regretted it. It has its standards, and it has its near-full capacity, and one lost Halston, a New York celebrity, wouldn't have upset the Beverly Hills. But once in a while there are some new guests for whom the hotel is happy to alter its standards—new guests the hotel doesn't want to lose.

§   §   §   §   §   §   §   §   §   §

They walked in off the street, so, really, who was to know?

He had a rough-and-tumble face that had been around. She was incredibly beautiful. Brigitte Bardot, in fact, had once said she was *the* most beautiful woman in the world.

They were Jean-Paul Belmondo and Ursula Andress. Quite innocently they arrived without a reservation, but being who they were, having been in the movies they had, with the exposure they had had, and based on past experiences at the world's finest hotels, they didn't think there would be a problem getting accommodations at this particular inn.

Who was to believe that even though they were two of the most often-photographed people in the world, no one at the front desk recognized their faces or their names?

The Beverly Hills, with rare exception, takes no "off the street" traffic. You must be vouched for, at the very least by your bank.

Belmondo was out of the conversation. He spoke no English. Andress did, but the proper words weren't coming out of her mouth—such as whom she knew in Hollywood and whether they would validate her.

Very firmly, the clerk was saying, "Sorry." But rather than make some terrible mistake—after all, these pople might be Somebodies—he asked them to take a seat over near the fireplace, while he checked them out.

After several calls, and not a few wishes that the foreign couple would just disappear, someone in the public-relations department finally recognized them. Room was quickly found, and Belmondo and Andress were quickly escorted to their suite by an assistant manager.

§ § § § § § § § § §

For most guests, the staff is a faceless group that, with an exception here and there, are anonymous. They do their job, and in the case of the Beverly Hills, they do it meticulously, and then they vanish.

Comedian and actor Henry Gibson tested this anonymity once while researching a part for a TV movie. He was to play a bellman in *Honeymoon Suite,* an inconsequential offering from ABC, set in a hotel.

To gain a feel for the role, Gibson worked a shift at the Beverly Hills. Among those he served while making $17.50 in tips were Howard Cosell and Mel Brooks, but no one recognized Gibson, who, if he hadn't been recognizable after reciting poetry on *Laugh-In* certainly was following his country-Western role in Robert Altman's *Nashville.*

While carrying out his appointed rounds, Gibson delivered some shirts to bungalow 3, where David Frost chatted with him about who else was staying at the hotel, Frost's defunct talk show, and other items of trivia and importance.

A scant two hours later Gibson, out of uniform and in civvies, ran into Frost again, this time in the lobby. Now Frost recognized him, talked shop for a while, and went on.

"I didn't tell him I was the bellman who delivered the shirt. It might have embarrassed him," Gibson told *Los Angeles Times* television writer Cecil Smith. "But it proved a point. In that uniform, people don't see you. They look right through you. Now, I've known David for years; I've been on his show several times. He looked me right in the eye when I was wearing that uniform and didn't know me.

Once out of the uniform and in my regular clothes, he recognized me instantly. Maybe I should have recited a poem."

Smith wanted to know how much Frost had tipped.

"That's another reason I didn't mention it. He stiffed me."

§   §   §   §   §   §   §   §   §   §

Some 500 people work at the Beverly Hills, serving 275 guests in 315 rooms. There are 21 switchboard operators, 30 kitchen workers, 16 bellmen, 10 full-time gardeners, desk clerks, managers, maids, waiters, porters. They are all people with curiosity, people with eyes and ears, people who gossip, just like anyone else. But their quiet efficiency often lulls guests into forgetting they are more than the furnishings. In front of the staff, guests will reveal things about themselves and what they do, things they would hide from anyone else.

§   §   §   §   §   §   §   §   §   §

Cosmetics queen Estée Lauder was quite the anathema among the staff. She was pushy and overbearing, and her tips weren't large enough to make up for her high-handedness.

In one sense Lauder was an egalitarian. She mistreated everyone equally. Until, that is, she had a run-in with Maude the Maid.

Maude was just a body to Lauder, a thing to be given orders. A gofer, a servant, a menial. Which was all fine and good until one day her tone of voice and manner proved too much for Maude.

"Listen, you hussy," the maid who had been watching said to the guest who had never noticed. "Don't be telling me what to do—you who sleep in this room with your husband and that room with your boyfriend."

It had never occurred to Lauder that something as inconsequential as Maude the Maid would be privy to that information.

From then on, Lauder always showed up with little gifties for Maude, samples from the newest line of lipsticks or powders. All the rest of the staff, however, were handled without care, as usual.

§   §   §   §   §   §   §   §   §   §

Gina Lollobrigida had arrived with her secretary. After a couple of days, the actress-photographer announced she wanted the secretary in a room nearer her own.

At the busy Beverly Hills, jockeying rooms is a complicated undertaking, but her request was answered with "Of course, Miss Lollobrigida. We will see that your secretary is moved as soon as possible."

The next day the secretary was put into the room adjoining her employer's.

Lollobrigida was back at the desk, her Latin temper showing.

Too close! Too close! Near but not the very room next to hers.

The secretary had to be moved again, and Lollobrigida was complaining again. Now the secretary was too far. And on it went.

Having heard of Lollobrigida's tantrums, it was with much relish that one of the maids made a report to the desk a few days later: "You know that terrible Italian woman who causes the trouble? Well, let me tell you, she hasn't got a hair on her whole head. She wears a wig."

§   §   §   §   §   §   §   §   §   §

Maids, quite naturally, are ones to notice personal habits and cleanliness.

Maude, for one, was always infuriated with Elizabeth

Taylor. She would come back from bungalow 3, the one National Velvet shared with Husband Four, Eddie Fisher, sputtering with indignation. Every morning Maude would come in and find a trail of clothes the two discarded, starting at the door, going through the living room and into the bedroom. The bathroom would have all of Taylor's numerous makeup vials, wands, and brushes scattered around it as if a cyclone had hit Bloomingdale's cosmetics counter. Sometimes there would be smudges of lipstick on the ceiling, although Maude never could figure out how they got there.

The dining-room table was no neater. Its top was invisible for half-empty bottles of liquor, jars of vitamin pills, and diamond bracelets, earrings, and rings, all of which Liz had flung higgledy-piggledy.

"It's a miracle," Maude would say, "a miracle they keep any of that jewelry, the way she takes care of it."

But it was mostly the dogs Maude objected to. In the confusion of her life, Taylor had neglected to train them properly. Occasionally, more like whenever they felt like it, the dogs wet the bed. The smell became so bad that the mattress had to be thrown out. (Taylor was charged for it.)

§ § § § § § § § § §

Bellmen have more personal, direct relationships with guests than do maids. When they are escorting one who doesn't rate the escort of a desk clerk or assistant manager, casual conversation often starts.

"It certainly is lovely weather for a vacation."

"Oh, I'm here on business."

"Really? What do you do?" And so on. You'd be surprised how much information is divulged in such chit-chat.

Bellmen are also the after-hours suppliers. If a guest wants liquor, the bellmen have a supply in their little room across from the front desk. Should a Big Mac attack hit, bellmen hurry off into the night to the nearest fast-food stand. (A hamburger and a malted could run twenty-five dollars if it's late enough.)

Since many of the bellmen, like most of the staff, have been there for years and years, they can remember a lot of people way back when—like Barbra Streisand, way back when she was second fiddle to Liberace's piano.

When Streisand was just starting out, the hotel personnel, including Alberto, a Cuban bellman, watched with amusement as she would walk through the lobby, hoping, agonizing over the wonderful possibility that someone might recognize her. In those days she found autographing a far-from-onerous task.

One day she sauntered into the lobby on the arm of her husband, Elliott Gould, fanning herself with something that had to have come from a thrift shop on Second Avenue. With all the demureness of Ethel Merman belting "Everything's Coming up Roses," Streisand announced to the bellmen, the desk clerks, most of the lobby, and some of the Polo Lounge, that her rooms were to be watched at all times be-cause she was afraid someone might steal her die-monds, which she couldn't, ya-know, put in the hotel safe, be-cause, things dis-appear from hotel safes.

Despite Streisand's hitting the big, big time, Alberto, at least, never forgot her posturings when her name was under Liberace's on the bill. Nor was he one to let her forget that he remembered.

A chance came when Streisand was supposed to appear at a Golden Globes presentation. She was sharing top box-office honors with Newman, Redford, and Wayne.

Streisand was three hours late.

"You're late," Alberto trumpeted when she finally appeared in the lobby. "You're late, and shame on you. Why, I remember when you were always the first one to arrive."

It was a long while after that before Streisand could

walk unhesitantly into the lobby. She never knew when Alberto would strike. Instead she took to driving her car into the garage and ascertaining by house phone Alberto's exact whereabouts.

§   §   §   §   §   §   §   §   §   §

Most hotels have direct dial. Around each number on the phone are dial instructions: 8 for long distance; 9 for local calls; 112, front desk; 115 room service; 118 valet, or what have you.

The Beverly Hills has clung to the more personal operator service, although it is bowing to "progress"with direct dial being installed in the fall of 1978.

The twenty-one operators placed all calls; took messages; left messages for you at other numbers; tracked down people for you in the Polo Lounge, at the pool, in Chasen's. An advertising executive, impressed by the operators, proclaimed them queens for the day and sent them all roses.

Some guests were never enraptured by the old system, complaining that it was less efficient than direct dial and that they sometimes had to wait to get a call out. Or sometimes had to wait to get a call in.

Some were also bothered by the operators' knowing who you're calling, and who was calling you.

Take the item in *New West* magazine, the *New York* of Southern California, that appeared in February 1978:

> When Columbia Pictures Industries president Alan Hirschfield flew out to Los Angeles the week before David Begelman resigned [for forging checks—and getting nailed by Cliff Robertson—while he was a Columbia executive] he didn't move into the bungalow at the Beverly Hills Hotel where he usually stays. Instead, Hirschfield sought refuge at L'Ermitage, a fashionable new hotel. Hirschfield wasn't saying why he avoided the big pink house on the hill, but one of his friends had an idea. "There have always been

rumors," the friend explained, "that Rona Barrett gets in-formation from the switchboard operators there."

Without question the switchboard operators knew what was up with Lionel Bart.

Lionel Bart was a composer, fond of black leather, who was getting first-class treatment from Columbia. Bart had written the Broadway hit *Oliver!* and Columbia was footing his bills while he was in town working on the movie version.

What they did not know, however, but could have if they had only asked the Beverly Hills switchboard operators, was that after Bart left each day for the studio, six or seven of his newfound boyfriends would show up at his suite. Bart kept asking the front desk for new keys and handing them out to new friends, until ten were in circulation.

The boys were having a wonderful time calling all their friends—New York, London, Seattle. They had a lot of friends, too. The phone bill was averaging two hundred dollars a day.

It didn't take Columbia's accounting office long to take exception to footing the two-hundred-dollar-a-day phone bills. They so informed Bart. Bewildered, he went to the hotel front office to complain about these mysterious charges, which after all, how could he be making, since he was away at the studio?

The switchboard solved the mystery. The calls might not have been Bart's, but when the bills had started mounting, they had listened in, and knew they were made by the kiddie brigade.

It did not come as much of a surprise, a few years later, when Bart declared bankruptcy.

"He should have put a lock on his phone," one Beverly Hills employee commented.

§ § § § § § § § § §

So the bellmen know if you're a late-night junk-food junkie. The maids know if you're sleeping alone. The cashiers know what you're spending and what you are allowed to spend. The switchboard keeps tabs on your calls. The kitchen knows what you eat. The cocktail lounge knows what you drink. And the valet knows the state of your clothes. The word got passed that although Johnny Carson might have his own line of clothes, that didn't keep his underwear from being holey.

§ § § § § § § § § §

Donald W. Curtis is the chairman of the Canadian Pacific Hotels, a few of which are in the luxury class. He was asked what he thought made a great hotel.

"You can have a great staff and moderate facilities and still have a great hotel, but you can have great facilities and moderate service, and you will not have a great hotel."

§ § § § § § § § § §

Of course, a staff is not some faceless, anonymous blob, automatons programmed to serve and nothing more. The staff is composed of individuals, with all the frailties, complexities, eccentricities, and complicated histories of any group of individuals. They have the same needs, desires, and interests, they have the same feuds, and they jockey and maneuver as employees of any other corporation do. Some of them are crazy. Some of them are sane. Some of them are a mixture of the two. Just like anywhere else.

The upper-level feuding and jockeying, back stabbing and triumphs are the most visible. They are the full-blown court intrigues, with the kingdom as the prize.

The kingdom, of course, is Silberstein's, but before his son-in-law rose to power, the question of who was to be his lord chancellor, who sat at his side, was a matter of contention for years.

When Silberstein had the lock, stock, and barrel in 1958, one of his first moves was to promote Stewart Hathaway to executive vice-president and to keep him on as manager.

Silberstein liked Hathaway's style, the hair grayed in the perfect places, the immaculate gray suits, the courtliness. Hathaway projected an image that Silberstein liked. Hathaway even lined up desk clerks each day to check the shines on their shoes and the creases in their pants.

But some say he failed in one very important respect. He didn't manage to lure the Old Guard, the Main Line Philadelphians, the proper Bostonians, or the Palm Beach and Greenwich, Connecticut, crowd to the hotel. They were who Silberstein wanted. He wanted the old rich, the Pasadenans, who continued to prefer the tiny Bel-Air.

The Gospel according to Management says Hathaway was moved upstairs to a seat on the board of directors because "as happens to all of us, Stewart grew older."

His obvious successor was Wallie Durden, who had been with the hotel for years. Durden was a social creature with a social wife, Jewell Curtis Cohn, a niece of the former Columbia Pictures dictator Harry Cohn.

Indeed, Durden did get promoted to manager, but to his dismay, being manager didn't mean what it had used to. He wasn't running the hotel; instead, he was a glorified desk man.

The real power had slipped past him into the hands of an outsider, Martin Rubin, a money man lured by Silberstein from the United California Bank, to be financial vice-president.

It must have been a letdown for Durden, to be manager and yet not to be, but as one observer noted, "He wasn't a qualified hotel man" to begin with, and the Beverly Hills Hotel was no place for on-the-job manager training.

Despite the nothingness of the job, Durden stayed on.

His wife had money, and his title had prestige. Durden had his own house account, which meant free wining and dining of his society friends. A very nice fringe benefit for a social type like him.

His playboy whirl proved his downfall. In 1969, according to insiders, Silberstein noticed something disturbing.

Durden and Jewell were getting more publicity than the hotel. That wouldn't do. A manager shouldn't be more famous than what he was managing.

Besides, Silberstein supposedly had never liked Jewell. She somehow always had a word of advice here, a suggestion there. She liked to run things from a banquette in the Polo Lounge. But worse, she had a piercing voice that could be heard clear from one end of the room to the other. Her voice did not belong at the Beverly Hills Hotel.

So one day, rather suddenly to bystanders but not unexpectedly to insiders, Silberstein heaved-ho Durden.

"With barely more than a whistle," says one employee who shall remain nameless, "Durden was gone."

(Not entirely forgotten, however. Durden popped up at the Fountainebleau in Miami Beach and then got in touch with his former secretary, still at the Beverly Hills. He had her forward Beverly Hills computer printouts of guest lists—including their home addresses. He then sent these guests little notes about how nice it was to have known them while he was in California, but since he had transferred the wonderful hospitality to Miami, why didn't they "come on down"?

(The secretary played Mata Hari until suspicions were aroused and a trap was set. She got caught with the print-outs in hand, and out she went also.)

It was now Rubin's show, to the dismay of some of the employees.

They feared he would change the character of the hotel by instituting parsimonious policies, just as he watched costs by crossing out overtime on their time cards. What if Rubin started cutting costs, pinching pennies when it came to guest services, turned the Beverly Hills into a Holiday Inn with parking attendants?

Rubin, a smiling Mr. Steel, gave the employees other reasons to dislike him as well.

§   §   §   §   §   §   §   §   §   §

Rubin told the employee in his office off the downstairs arcade to wait a minute. He had a long-distance call to make.

As it turned out it was to a woman who had worked for the hotel for thirteen years. She was vacationing.

"Hello," the Beverly Hills end of the conversation went. "This is Mr. Rubin at the hotel. . . . I'm fine. . . . Yes, about your vacation. You needn't bother coming back. You're fired. . . . Yes, that will be all taken care of. Goodbye."

The employee with Rubin sat in disbelief as the hotel vice-president chuckled.

"I hated to ruin her vacation, but that's when I usually tell people they're fired, when they are on vacation."

This man is a gem, the employee thought to himself.

§   §   §   §   §   §   §   §   §   §

There are various versions of what caused Rubin's downfall.

The official one, the one Slatkin expounds, is that he wasn't doing his job. No court intrigues. No rivalry with Slatkin, the son-in-law.

Rubin "was terminated after seven years because of a growing difference in policy matters between Silberstein and him."

In fact, says Slatkin, he asked Silberstein not to fire Rubin and was sorry to see him go.

But others have said that Rubin's departure greatly pleased Muriel, whose husband was now to have a clear field.

Rubin's downfall was swift but not sudden. Silberstein picked a fight with him one day, and threw him out before the ex-vice-president had time to collect his pencils.

After his hasty dismissal, Rubin tried an Hernando Courtright. He decided to compete with the Beverly Hills. First, however, he went down to San Diego to a hotel owned by one of Richard Nixon's moneyed buddies. When the buddy ran into trouble with the IRS, Rubin came back to Los Angeles and got involved with Carriage House in Westwood, a hotel that was intended to give the Beverly Hills and the Wilshire a run for the Mercedes trade. Insiders say that with a few more millions and a few more years, Rubin might have been able to pull it off. But in the end he and his backers sold out. The Carriage House is now the Sunset Hyatt House.

Rubin, a fairly wealthy man himself, is now playing golf.

Burton Slatkin is now running the Beverly Hills Hotel. Which once again probably goes to show that blood is thicker than the ink on business-school diplomas.

§   §   §   §   §   §   §   §   §   §

That's the upstairs. The downstairs at the court may not be as Machiavellian, but it has its share of stories and people and, of couse, names to know.

Hollis Polodna, for one,

His is that signature at the bottom of your letter of confirmation.

Polodna was the man who thoughtfully assigned Margaret Truman, on her 1972 visit, the same room she had occupied in 1950, when, as first daughter, she sang in the Hollywood Bowl.

Because of his power-wielding room assignments, Polodna is a well-tipped man.

Bill Bixby, the assistant reservation manager, will never take a tip handed directly over the counter but is still extensively Guccied.

At the front desk during the day there is Nick Pappas, the assistant day manager.

At one time Pappas lived in a tiny room in the hotel—free room, free meals. He had moved in after a trying divorce. Silberstein offered the room. He could understand trying divorces.

At night there is Ernie Brown, a twenty-five-year veteran who sometimes brings in his black, silver-flecked standard poodle, Tina, to help man the desk.

Assistant managers are in charge of the two clerks on duty with them. The clerks' duties, if a job prospectus was to be written, includes typing out information cards on arriving guests, making out another slip in triplicate (one is immediately plopped down a pneumatic tube to the switchboard so they can address you by name when you pick up the phone), and preparing a folio for the cashier's office. Usually the room assignment will have been pre-decided by someone higher up. But less-desirable rooms will be given out by clerks.

Beyond that, the prospectus would read that clerks give out keys, sort mail into boxes, hand it out, and answer questions and the phone.

But as with most jobs, there's more to it than the prospectus would state.

For one thing, there's the diplomatic assignment of handling the crazies on the phone—like Steve McQueen looking for Ali McGraw or the late-night drunks who need someone, anyone, to talk to. David Janssen is one late-nighter. He wants desperately to talk about anything from the weather to the World Series as long as there's an ear pressed to the other end of the line.

Guests solicit the clerk's advice on what to wear.

"Well, I'm going to a cocktail party in the Hills. Do you think it will be terribly formal or do you always dress out here?"

Or Roy Cohn, looking intimidated as he checks in and asking the bellman where to eat and how to dress for the hotel restaurants.

Wives without husbands call for help in buttoning buttons, and husbands without wives are constantly needing assistance with their ties.

"I must have tied a thousand ties," says one former clerk. "Guys who have no idea how to tie a tie because their wives always tie for them. Incredible."

Simone Signoret had one favorite bellman. "Please, I need help," she'd phone in. "I'm up at some place in the hills and I don't know how to get back. Would you come and get me?"

Ernie Brown was approached with a "little problem" once.

A German baroness, a member of the Krupp armaments family, was missing a bag.

Without much concern or anxiety, she explained to Brown that the airline had apparently misplaced it.

She ordinarily wouldn't bother Brown with this matter, but, well, "I have all my jewelry in that bag. I forgot to carry it as I usually do, and put it in the suitcase. I've never lost a suitcase before."

Somewhere, in some city serviced by the airline, was the baroness's three million dollars' worth of jewels.

Brown raced to the airport and spent most the night having a trace put on the bag. Miraculously, it turned up in Rio de Janeiro and was quickly returned to the Baroness.

Next to where the clerks work, around the bend of the front desk, are the cashier's cages. Two work per shift, and then an auditor-cashier takes over at graveyard time.

Some cashiers come and go, and others seem to stay on forever. One of the latter was a sixtyish woman who didn't have to work. Her family had money, allowing her to be casual about such details as working hours. At one time this cashier had commandeered four of the hotel's safe-deposit boxes—one for stocks and bonds, another for cash, a third for jewelry, and the last for her insurance policies.

Finally someone worked up enough nerve to say, "Gee, I

think our guests would like to use a safe—couldn't you give up at least one?" She was probably the only cashier to literally wash her pencils, and if she didn't like a particular guest, she simply stuck a CLOSED sign on her window until the guest was gone.

Another cashier kept picking the wrong boyfriends. That shouldn't have affected her job, but she also kept cashing her boyfriends' checks. She would make good when they bounced, over a period of time. Then one day, the current amour's check was big and bounced too high. And the cashier was out.

Another cashier, striking in a Brooklyn Barbra way, had the rest of the front staff mystified. She kept disappearing into the ladies' room all the time. She looked healthy, and she didn't come back tipsy—as one did; everyone knew she had had a nip when her breath smelled like cloves—so no one could figure out the puzzle.

Solution time came when this cashier came whizzing in a few minutes late one morning. In her hurry she didn't notice that the floor had just been waxed. Up flew her feet, she was down, and her wig was off. The woman, completely bald, was always running to the bathroom to adjust her hairpiece.

A pastime of the more romantic cashiers is to check out the status of handsome male guests.

"Well, do you think this is a good one? See what he does." They check out his history and fantasize a little.

The cashier with the poor romantic track record was not the only employee to have to settle a debt with the hotel. A food checker in the kitchen—her job is to see that the proper food is on the proper trays, that the food is warm, that the bill is totaled correctly—had something of a drinking problem. One night after work, in backing her car out of the employee garage space, she managed to run over the hotel's gas pump. The damage was in the tens of thousands, which got paid back chunk by chunk out of her paycheck, over many years.

§ § § § § § § § § §

Any organization is going to have its stars. Of the two employees who stand out most at the Beverly Hills, one isn't an employee at all. He is Leon Smith, but who knows him by that name? He's Smitty. The tall, uniformed fixture at the end of the porte cochere. He doesn't work for the hotel because he owns the parking-lot concession.

Smith started parking cars at the Beverly Hills when he was sixteen years old, in 1939.

"I never thought I'd stay," he said a few years ago, "when I came to park cars at night and work in a service station during the day." In the best Horatio Alger tradition, Smitty went from parking boy to partner and then with some associates to owner of the concession, which is leased from the hotel.

Smitty is a man to be cultivated. It's extra status points when your car shows up faster than others from the lot, because you are obviously a friend of Smitty's. People gladly give generously to earn Smitty's friendship, to be able to abandon their cars without waiting for a claim check, and to have someone go for their cars as soon as they emerge from the hotel.

The other highly visible employee is easily remembered because he isn't highly visible.

Buddy Douglas is a midget who for twenty-four years has been wandering the lobby and the Polo Lounge yelling, "Ca-ll for Mistah Silvah-man" or "Ca-ll for Carroll O'Conn-ah" in the very same way he used to yell, "Ca-ll for Phil-lip Mo-rris."

§ § § § § § § § § §

The staff watches as they work. They are amused by some of the happenings, saddened by others, and once in a while they are awed.

They see it all. They know it all.

Chapter Eight

What a perfect spot for an assignation.
—Aldous Huxley, surveying a lanai-patio at the
Beverly Hills Hotel

romances . . .

It certainly didn't start out as an assignation.

They were co-workers, artistes-in-arms, each chummy with the other's spouse.

But then the wife left for Italy to make her own picture, and the husband for New York because great plays don't grow in Southern California soil. And they were alone.

At the Beverly Hills Hotel.

In adjoining bungalows.

She was lonely, and he was frustrated as he saw his part being whittled to nothing.

And the Beverly Hills is a perfect spot for an assignation.

They moved into bungalow 10 together.

She was Marilyn Monroe, disorganized, insecure, the blonde incarnation of worldly innocence. *Let's Make Love* was to be her twenty-seventh film. Critics had begun to change opinions of Monroe after her performances in *Bus Stop* and *Some Like It Hot*. No longer was she just a no-talent in a low-cut dress whose walk, as Jerry Lewis once described it, looked like two puppies fighting under a blanket. Now she was a comedienne of talent.

Marilyn was no newcomer at the Beverly Hills. She had lounged around the pool hoping for the Big Break. She had made the party scene in the ballrooms. Had been paged at the Polo Lounge. Wiggled through the lobby. Done the starlet routine.

The difference with Marilyn, what set her apart from the other near-pathetic, eager young actresses dying to be seen, is that people did notice her, especially after she got her weak chin fixed.

At a party, given by *Look* magazine in the early 1950s, Sheilah Graham's boss, a man with an inclination for blondes, spotted Marilyn across the room. He, as President Sukarno had, wanted to know who *that* was.

"Oh, a new starlet," Graham had dismissed her, as many women had in the early days. Men couldn't. The boss had to meet her.

"You are very pretty," he told Marilyn, "and you'll be a great success."

Of course, she was.

Not that he, Yves Montand, wasn't. Montand was a star, all right, but not in the United States, where, at that particular moment to him, it seemed to count.

Montand was a music-hall man, a singer, or more precisely an interpreter of song, a former protégé and lover of Edith Piaf.

Let's Make Love, a silly fluff, was important to Montand.

When the film went into production, the two couples—Monroe and Arthur Miller, Montand and Simone Signoret—were ensconced at the back of the garden in bungalows 20 and 21, which are actually bungalow suites on the second floor of a two-story building. Today they cost $132 a night.

It was an easy enough existence in the beginning. Monroe and Montand would go off to the 20th Century lot early in the morning. Miller would coffee with Signoret while discussing his day's work schedule.

In the evening, after shooting, the four would get together for an unwinding drink and sometimes for dinner. Once Marilyn and Signoret pooled utensils from their kitchenettes and twirled up a spaghetti repast.

When Monroe had time off, she gravitated to Signoret, a woman she couldn't help admiring. Monroe had been told so often that she was a body and no talent. Signoret, on the other hand, was a recognized actress. The odds were that Signoret would get an Academy Award nomination that year for *Room at the Top*. (Not only did she get the nomination, but she took home the statue as well.)

The two went shopping together and together had their hair dyed by a little old lady who claimed to have been Jean Harlow's hair colorist.

Then Signoret left. She went to Italy to film *Adua et Ses Compagnes*.

Miller left.

And Montand's part was chipped, scraped, and reduced. As more lines were taken from him, his moroseness increased.

Add this frustration to his not being immune to the charms of ladies other than his wife, and there might have been an affair anyway anywhere.

But Monroe and Montand weren't *any*where. They were at the Beverly Hills, the intoxicating, bawdy, dream-built, passionate, erotic Beverly Hills Hotel, with its gardens reeking with sex and scented with romance. Tropical, sultry, pure, and innocent.

Montand and Monroe had their affair.

And the press had its picnic.

Until the picture began to wind down. Then Montand began packing his bags to return to Signoret, as he always did, because the affairs always ended. The marriage did not.

An idyllic little dalliance then turned ugly. The fights began. One night Monroe locked her lover out. He banged on the door, finally breaking it down. She meanwhile had got a call through to the cops. It was all very embarrassing and took a lot of hushing up, or at least toning down. Montand moved back to his own bungalow.

Marilyn started her calls. She had to talk to him. He didn't want to talk to her. The switchboard operators felt sorry for Monroe. It was all so sad.

Before Montand was able to make his escape from Southern California, he got a visit from columnist Hedda Hopper, who after years of peeping into others' lives felt qualified to hand out advice on how to live them.

Signoret, in her autobiography, gently disputes Hopper's version of what ensued. Montand, she contends, didn't speak English well enough to have said what Hopper claims.

"It can't be true," Signoret writes, "if for no other reason than by its grammatical form and its difficulties of pronunciation it would cost Montand a week's hard work."

Be that as it may, as Hopper tells it, she went swooping down on Montand at his bungalow, like an indignant angel. As he invited her in, the phone rang.

"No," he told the operator, "I still won't speak to her. I won't take the call."

"Why not?" Hopper demanded. "You'll probably never see her again. Go on. Speak to her."

He wouldn't. So between sips of martini, Hopper scolded him. Didn't Montand know that Monroe was "unsophisticated," an innocent? How could you lead her down this primrose path? How could you be so cruel?

"Had Monroe been sophisticated," Montand was supposed to have answered, "none of this ever would have happened. I did everything I could for her when I realized mine was a very small part. The only thing I could stand out in my performance were my love scenes. So, naturally, I did everything I could to make them good! . . . Perhaps she had a schoolgirl's crush. If she did, I'm sorry. But nothing will break up my marriage."

The same could not be said for Monroe's. She and Miller were divorced soon after.

Let's Make Love was a bomb, although some critics liked the love scenes.

§   §   §   §   §   §   §   §   §   §

"The Beverly Hills Hotel is a wonderful place to start a love affair," says Jon Fast, author, would-be screenwriter, son of Howard *Spartacus* Fast, lover and now husband of Erica *Fear of Flying* Jong.

He should know.

That's where he and Jong got together.

§   §   §   §   §   §   §   §   §   §

Between husband number three John Huston and husband number four Artie Shaw, Evelyn Keyes took up with Mike Todd.

Or rather, the flamboyant Mr. Todd took up with her. He was captivated, enraptured with this glorious, intelligent woman who had played Mrs. Mike and Ruby Keeler in *The Jolson Story*. In his extravagantly fulgent manner, he decided it was only a question of *when* they would have an affair.

There was no question of *where*.

As Keyes tells it in her autobiography, *Scarlett O'Hara's Younger Sister*, after a couple of navy grogs at Trader Vic's to smooth the rough edges, Todd took her back to a suite at the Beverly Hills Hotel. Management had kindly furnished a basket of fruit, and Todd had kindly furnished a chilled bottle of Dom Perignon.

A wonderful place to start a love affair, even a roller-coasting one like that of Keyes and Todd.

Theirs lasted, up and down, side to side, back and forth, for several years and over a couple of continents, but they often drifted back to that spot where they had first got it on.

At one point, when Todd was in Venice, and Keyes on her way to Hawaii, Sheilah Graham asked her when the wedding date would be announced.

"Oh, Sheilah, I'm not marrying Mike or anybody else just now. Don't you think I've done enough of that sort of thing to last me awhile?" (She had already "I do-ed" it three times.)

The quote was published. Todd read it in Europe.

Telegram to Keyes: "So you don't want to marry me why am I the last to know?"

Back to the Beverly Hills, where Hedda Hopper, always full of her good counsel, told Keyes to marry the man.

The man showed up and took Keyes to the Polo Lounge, at quiet time, midafternoon.

After ordering "a lemonade with two straws," he gave her a flower pin carved in old ivory, petaled with sapphires and diamonds. But the problems they were having weren't to be solved with a gift. Keyes had pretty well decided to use her airline reservation and move to Paris.

She wrote, "He took the reservation out of my hand and slipped it into his pocket. 'I'll turn it in. . . . I tried, it didn't work, I can't . . . we got to try again, I'm . . . your fella, what can I do . . .?' "

What could they do but head upstairs to a suite?

It was reconciliation at the Beverly Hills.

The reconciliation didn't last, of course. Todd met Elizabeth Taylor. Was captivated, enraptured by her.

They were married and lived happily ever after until his plane, *The Lucky Liz*, crashed, killing him and everyone else on board.

§   §   §   §   §   §   §   §   §   §

Paul Newman and Joanne Woodward couldn't afford assignations at the Beverly Hills Hotel before they were married.

They can now.

So they do.

Check in. Order wine, beer, gourmet munchies. Tell the switchboard operator to hold all calls.

They did this even when they had their own Beverly Hills home a few blocks away.

§   §   §   §   §   §   §   §   §   §

Wide-eyed, breathless, violins-in-the-background trysts, of the Gable-Lombard variety, are contrasted by the mundane, earthy, slightly sleazo, hot and panting types.

The privacy of the hotel, the accessibility to the bungalows and rooms without being seen, without having to go through the lobby, all the side entrances and the many garden paths, lend themselves to quickies and nooners and fast ones behind the matey's back.

Some lotharios-about-town are regular nooners. Take the room for an hour with the girl of the day, tousle the sheets, and check out. But many times they never check in. They have pull with one or another of the executives. Their names never appear in the guest rack, and no one is supposed to be the wiser or have access to incriminating or, at the very least, embarrassing evidence.

Of course, nooners invariably slip up. They'll sign a room-service chit without thinking. Or they'll make a telephone call, a giveaway to the switchboard. Or they'll be spotted on the way out by a maid, making beds in another room with the door slightly ajar.

Greg Bautzer, lawyer and one-time good buddy to Howard Hughes, and producer Bob Evans are nooners of note.

Although it may come as a shock to some, Eli Robbins has been known to noon.

Robbins is a fixture in the Polo Lounge, Every day, at the same time, he takes his place at a table, a red carnation as his boutonniere.

Every couple of weeks, after lunch, Robbins repairs with a lovely to a room.

The two don't play canasta, either. The maids report, "Yup, it's not for show."

Robbins is in his nineties.

§   §   §   §   §   §   §   §   §   §

Songwriter Jule Styne, though not a nooner like Robbins, has a set routine also.

Whenever he is arriving from the East Coast, a woman, always very attractive, arrives an hour before Stein to pick up his room key. Two hours after he checks in, the woman reappears in the lobby on her way out.

§   §   §   §   §   §   §   §   §   §

As has been noted earlier, JFK had a hideaway room at the Beverly Hills. He'd register somewhere else or be staying with friends, but at the same time he would be slipping off with his array of girlfriends, from Angie Dickinson and Monroe to a famous French skier, all with the Secret Service's knowledge, of course.

Phyllis Kirk, an actress who had once starred in the TV version of *The Thin Man* with Jack's brother-in-law Peter Lawford, showed up uninvited at JFK's bungalow door. She had been introduced to Kennedy previously, not by Lawford, but by her about-to-be-estranged husband, comedian Mort Sahl.

When Kennedy, always the politician, asked, "How's Mort?" Kirk came back with "How should I know? I'm not his keeper. I'm a person too."

Her answer was flaky enough that Kennedy wanted nothing further to do with her. She was probably one of the few attractive females to whom he gave the fast rush—out.

marriages . . .

It's not the happy marriages that get noticed, it's the ones that are the nothing more than first phase in divorce proceedings.

Who could help but notice the night Robert Wagner and

his wife, between the marriages to Natalie Wood, had their battle in the lobby?

They had attended one of the large, costly galas that are always being thrown at the hotel. On the way out it was quite obvious that some difference of opinion had arisen between them.

"You're not going home with me!" she screamed.

"You're so right!" he agreed, and promptly asked for the best suite available. Wife huffed out to the car and peeled away. Husband went upstairs to bed.

"At least they were in a hotel," was the comment at the desk.

§   §   §   §   §   §   §   §   §   §

It's got so nobody expects Zsa Zsa (née Sari) Gabor's marriages to last. This concerns husband number—oh, who counts any more?—businessman Herbert Hutton. He and Zsa Zsa had checked into a one-bedroom suite.

No sooner had Hutton left the building on some errand, than Zsa Zsa was on the phone to the front desk.

"Dahlings, there's been a mistake. We vant a two-bedroom sveet."

"No problem, Miss Gabor—that is, Mrs. Hutton—we'll move you right away." Which was all well and good—until Herbie came back.

"What is this!" he demanded. "I don't want a two-bedroom suite. Move us back to the other one, immediately." But Herbie was too late; there were no more one-bedrooms available.

For days, furious Herbie called the front desk, demanding to be moved. The situation was intolerable. Zsa Zsa was insisting on sleeping in separate bedrooms, locking hers to ensure that they did. Finally, a terrific racket came from the Hutton suite. Herbie had had enough—and apparently had also seen *Gone with the Wind.* He broke down the door.

As luck would have it, a one-bedroom suite was available the next day. The two moved in and lived happily ever after until the divorce. This is, after all, Zsa Zsa, the terror of the Carpathians, we're discussing.

§ § § § § § § § § §

A very chic American-born but French-looking woman checked in. She was Cappy Badrutt, an international society-column favorite who was married to André Badrutt, owner of the Palace Hotel and most of the rest of Saint Moritz.

She arrived with her son and maid, which caused a bit of a stir because very few people travel with maids any more, and no reservation, which also caused a bit of a stir. Professional courtesy being what it is—a favor from a hotelman to a hotelman—madame Badrutt moved into bungalow 3. Plus she rented one of the larger safes for her rather large jewel box.

If ever there was anyone who had adapted to the late-night-party routine, the high-society, jet-set existence, it was Cappy Badrutt.

She rarely stretched herself out of bed before cocktail time. A sleek, dark woman with the look of a pampered Burmese cat, she would arrive at the front desk in the evening to retrieve this or that of her jewels. There weren't many, but like her, they were beautiful—and very expensive.

Then it would be off to this event or that party, liqueurs with friends, and eventually back to the hotel.

Cappy's schedule left her young son and her maid to fend for themselves in Los Angeles, alone, during the day. In New York they could have walked to the zoo, taken in a museum, strolled on Fifth Avenue. In Los Angeles, they were trapped.

Cappy appealed to one of the friendlier desk clerks on the night shift—she rarely saw anyone on dayside. "I'm so tired of sending off my maid and my little boy in taxis. They have nothing to do but drive around the city all day."

Anyone who has been in the city in question knows that taking cabs is a bank-breaking proposition.

The clerk volunteered to take the two waifs to the beach during the day.

The boy loved it. In length, breadth, and beauty, California beaches are hard to match. While the boy built castles, the maid and the clerk practiced second languages on each other. The maid was Spanish; she spoke no English and a little French. The clerk was U.S.A.–born and –bred; he spoke no Spanish and a little French.

So it went, until Cappy started sending telegrams to Paris—in French. Very frustrating to the clerk and others on the desk who wanted to know what was going on. The French sessions at the beach weren't advanced enough to be much help.

Help and translation were sought from a French-Canadian cashier.

Telegram translation: "I've got away, *chéri*, and I miss you. Everything is all right now. We will meet in Las Vegas."

Telegrams from *chéri*, telegrams from Cappy. The desk was able to keep close tabs on Madame Badrutt's affair, for the telegrams were definitely not going home to Monsieur Badrutt.

Then she was gone, son, maid, and jewels, to the Tropicana in Las Vegas, the hotel built by questionable East Coast money, as opposed to the other strip hotels, which had been built with questionable West Coast money.

No sooner had they swirled off, than a message came over the Telex machine—for Ben Silberstein, from André Badrutt—a request for more professional courtesy.

Badrutt wanted his son, the maid, the jewel box. Cappy he didn't care about. Would Mr. Silberstein get in touch immediately?

Telegrams zinged from California, across the Atlantic to Saint Moritz, and back.

Silberstein turned to the staff for help. Did anyone have an inkling where son, maid, jewel box, and yes, Cappy were headed?

The friendly desk clerk, who knew the state, city, hotel, and room number, was mum. Everyone else was mum.

Without cooperation from his staff, Silberstein managed to track Cappy down to Las Vegas. Too late. She was gone.

More tracking to San Francisco, where Silberstein, no doubt through professional courtesy, got scent of her.

Cappy came back to the Beverly Hills, without her son, maid, and jewel box.

"What happened?" her friend the clerk wanted to know.

"Don't ask. I'm not sure. Some awful men came and grabbed my son. I don't know how André found out where I was."

The clerk had his suspicions but kept them to himself.

After a while Cappy left.

§   §   §   §   §   §   §   §   §   §

Cappy is no longer Madame Badrutt.

The staff wonders if Mrs. U.S. Olympic Team Coach has also joined the ranks of exes.

Mr. and Mrs. checked in together requesting twin beds in their room.

After a few days, the Mrs. left.

Call from the coach. He'd like the twin beds replaced with a king-size, if possible, a double if nothing larger was available.

No problem.

The beds were switched. Then who should arrive but the star of the coach's Olympic team—the *male* star?

They shared the room.

Call from the coach. He wanted the twins brought back.

Reswitch, and presto, the wife returned. The Olympic star moved into his own room.

triangles. . .

Prentis Cobb Hale and his wife, Marialice, could afford to be social butterflies. He was, after all, a Hale of the lucrative Broadway-Hale chain of department stores. They were prominent San Francisco Opera Association types.

When they extended their socializing to Los Angeles, the Beverly Hills Hotel was where they stayed. For one thing it was so convenient to their good friend Denise Minnelli.

Denise, a tiny wisp of a woman, was something of a social striver. Her house was catty-corner across Canon St. from the hotel. she used her address and her former alliance with director Vincente Minnelli, one of Judy Garland's exes, to further entrench herself in the social battleground.

Denise was always throwing parties and soirées and always looking for guests. She'd show up at the front desk with invitations to be sorted into the mailboxes. And if she'd happened to overlook someone important—someone like society columnist Suzy—Denise would scurry across the street in the middle of the night, dressed in nightgown and sunglasses, to make sure the important person got an invitation.

Physically they were an odd-shaped triangle. Prentis was robust, a boisterous fellow who looked as if any moment he would leap into his jodhpurs and be off chasing the hounds. Marialice was a big, matronly woman whose clothes never fell fashionably right. Standing next to Marialice, Denise looked even smaller and more delicate than she was. And they were such good friends.

Then came a night when Prentis left for a Denise party, but his wife stayed in the hotel.

A room-service waiter, on his way back to the kitchen

with a serving cart, heard an incongruous sound from the garden of the Beverly Hills. He heard weeping.

The sobs were from Mrs. Hale. She was hunched over the steps outside her bungalow.

"What's wrong, Mrs. Hale? Is there something I can do, something I can get you?"

The waiter was concerned. This was a woman he had waited on and chatted with for years. Not a friend, in any real sense, but a guest, his guest, and a person in distress.

"If only there were. There's nothing I can do. I've tried," Mrs. Hale wept.

The waiter didn't know what she was talking about, but it was clear she needed to unburden herself to someone.

"It's that awful woman. She's stealing my husband. What am I to do?"

There was nothing she could do on the bungalow steps, the waiter soothed her. Go inside. Lie down. Perhaps in the morning . . .

Denise threw another party, this time in celebration of Mrs. Hale's birthday.

Prentis went. Marialice stayed in the hotel.

On March 26, 1969, the headline in the *San Francisco Chronicle* read, MRS. PRENTIS COBB HALE KILLS HERSELF.

It happened in the family mansion. She shot herself, one .38-caliber bullet, directly through the head.

Prentis had spoken to her while she was getting ready for bed. Then he had gone downstairs to watch television.

"I heard one shot," he said. He raced upstairs, and there she was on the floor of his dressing room.

She had, he said, given no indication she would take her life.

Denise became the new Mrs. Hale.

§   §   §   §   §   §   §   §   §   §

The marriage was made in Perino's restaurant, not heaven.

There, says actress Victoria Sosa (you might have seen

her on *Fantasy Island*), she promised to love, honor, and obey the twenty-three-year-old son of Sheik Shamsuddin Abdullah.

Her sheik, Sheik Mohammed, has made a name for himself in Beverly Hills lately by making some interesting changes to the Sunset Boulevard mansion Shiek Daddy gave him.

He painted the house lime-green, plopped plastic flowers around the grounds, and decorated the genitalia of some statutes with highly visible colors.

Beverly Hillsians have not been amused, but they would have been surprised to learn what followed the ceremony at Perino's.

Sheik Mohammed already had a wife—four wives are permitted to a man under Islamic law—so he took bride Victoria elsewhere.

He took her, she claims, to a Beverly Hills hotel, where he beat her, attacked her sexually, and "bit her from shoulder to calf."

He kept her locked in the suite under guard for twenty-three days and wouldn't let her sleep without his permission.

She escaped, she said, when he and the guards fell asleep watching television.

Victoria is suing for five thousand dollars in general damages and ten million dollars in punitive damages.

A Beverly Hills hotel?

The Beverly Hills Hotel.

§   §   §   §   §   §   §   §   §   §

Pink Palace romances should have lightness and gossamer and fairy-tale beginnings.

Such as: Once upon a time there was a very terribly rich leader of the Rheingold Beer Company who used to visit the Pink Palace. When he arrived, he rented his coaches from Hertz.

He chose Hertz because it maintains a small office, really a counter, on the landing between the lobby and second floor.

That is where our very terribly rich Prince Charming found his Cinderella, who wore, in lieu of a glass slipper, the black-and-gold uniform of the car-rental chain.

Enchanted, Prince Rheingold changed his single for a double, whisked Cinderella Hertz from the drudgery of her counter, and married her.

divorces . . .

The privacy of the hotel, the quiet, mellow feeling that you don't have to hurry any faster than the butterflies drifting through the garden, makes the hotel a refuge of many sorts. It's a place for assignations, and it is also a place for divorces, a place to escape to when the going has become too rough, a place to go to sit down and pick up the pieces.

When you're leaving a mansion, a palace is a soothing retreat.

Barbara Carney has a major misunderstanding with her husband, Art, so she's into the Beverly Hills as fast as it takes to call reservations.

Monroe cloisters there after the breakup with Joltin' Joe Di Maggio, in 1954, because packs of photographers snap at her everywhere else.

Liz Taylor retreats to the Beverly Hills when her marriages dissolve.

In June 1976, Gwen Davis did a piece on Taylor for *McCall's* entitled, with understatement, "My Life Is a Little Complicated."

Davis wrote,

> We celebrated Elizabeth Taylor's 44th birthday in a Greek restaruant in Los Angeles. . . . Unfortunately, Elizabeth couldn't join us. She was in seclusion at the Beverly Hills Hotel.
>
> I saw her some weeks later at the Polo Lounge of the

Beverly Hills Hotel. She looked tired. I asked where she was going to go. "Oh, I'm just sort of hedgehopping," she said. . . .

Then, like the sound of a sorrowful trumpet, came the news, again, that Richard and Elizabeth were separating. [This was after their second stab at marriage.] She was on her way back to Hollywood. Henry [Wynberg] was waiting for her, of course. She didn't move in with him at first. She stayed some days hidden behind the palm fronds of the Beverly Hills Hotel, which was suddenly surrounded by teeny-boppers, who had hoped to catch a glimpse of a rock star until they found out "she" was there.

Those teenyboppers must have been Taylor's hair shirt. The hotel is adept at dispatching such unwanteds quickly enough. There is always a gaggle of gawkers lining the porte cochere on Sundays, with cameras growing from gaudy Hawaiian shirts. The gawkers are there, and permitted there, to catch a glimpse of Cher or Taylor or bionic people or Fonda or Stewart.

(Back in the Beatle-frenzied days, a pack of teenies were camped out at the entrance ramp, yearning for the Fab Four. They were willing to settle, in fact go delirious over, sighting the Beatles' manager, Brian Epstein.

(As the fans swooned over the pudgy dexedriner, Richard Arlen, one of those famous faces from an earlier era, waited patiently for his car to be brought up, completely ignored. His was a different time; fame had brushed him and moved on. His former swooners, by that time in their sixties, had outgrown such manifestations of adulation.)

Chapter Nine

and other hanky-panky . . .

Decorum drenches the Beverly Hills Hotel. Not the decorum of East Coast hotels, where the elevator men almost bow when you get into the car, or European hotels, where they literally do.

It's a less formal brand of decorum at the Beverly Hills, but striking nonetheless.

The place is permeated with a self-conscious sense of propriety, vigilantly maintained. An old-guard establishment, with old-guard sensibilities and no wish to change. For years the hotel has fought the dungaree mentality and still insists that at night men wear jackets in the Polo Lounge. Quaint, but not, as Dorothy Parker once sniffed, the place where elephants go to die.

You won't find rock stars hanging out in the bungalows, unless they can mind their manners.

The Beverly Hills doesn't want them. Its pink walls would have blushed scarlet if a madman like Jim Morrison ever carried on there. Morrison, lead singer with the Doors, was one of a triumvirate of influential rock stars who died at the beginning of the seventies—Janis Joplin, Jimi Hendrix, and Morrison.

Morrison, a certified beer-drinking freak who sang of

lighting your fire, was busted in Florida for flashing bare ass to his ecstatic concert audience. Morrison's appeal was his pre-punk unpredictability. During an interview with a writer he was buddying with, Morrison decided to do some calisthenics, on the ledge of his hotel balcony, ten stories above Sunset Boulevard.

The Beverly Hills would never permit such shenanigans.

§   §   §   §   §   §   §   §   §   §

Some call the Beverly Hills stuffy. The Beverly Hills calls itself well mannered.

It doesn't want rowdies and hooligans even if they contritely pay for damages.

As the hotel's public-relations man, Mal Sibley, explained, "The kind of people that would indicate a deposit required, we'd rather not have at all. In the case of people we've had problems with, there's no space available when they call."

The Crystal Room was damaged in 1976 when a rock entourage literally swung from the chandeliers. The havoc was extensive.

"Liquor and food were spilled all over the walls and the carpet," Sibley said, "which also had cigarette burns. There was broken furniture, a little bit of everything. They had a lot of fun, but it wasn't the kind of fun that we think is fun."

The revelers ended up paying thousands to repair their brand of fun.

Which isn't to say the Beverly Hills is completely intolerant of a bit of rambunctiousness and hasn't had some in her day.

Not the least was one party of Robert Mitchum's.

It all began, extemporaneously, when Mitchum found a good drinking friend in a tire executive from Dayton. They were in adjoining suites, so the two downed a few. And then a few more. And it seemed a shame not to spread the good-fellowship.

"Come on over; we're having a party." Before too many jiggles of the cocktail shaker, a full-fledged bash was going strong.

Jack Keith, a bellman who later parlayed his tips into a tavern on Wilshire Boulevard, remembered, "I worked there for six years, and I've seen plenty. I guess the wildest party has to be the four-day binge that Mitchum threw. . . . It had everything—booze, broads, and guys. It went on in two suites, Mitchum's and this other fellow's, which were together. All I can remember is everybody walked around in various stages of undress."

§   §   §   §   §   §   §   §   §   §

Some hijinks are tolerated with a smile. They add spice and ginger to the atmosphere. Who could help but be amused when Bobby and his swarm of Kennedy kids played tag and touch football from their cars, up the red carpet, into the lobby, and with a whirligig of commotion went out to their bungalows?

Or what of the scramble that ensued when the staff went in pursuit of an errant pet monkey that somehow managed to escape the Kennedy kids and Smith cousins? Finding the monkey was top priority. The little beast, it was feared, might sink its incisors into some innocent on her or his way into the Polo Lounge.

Not to be outdone by a passel of youngsters, Red Buttons misplaced his bush baby, a small African animal related to the lemur, in his laundry. An innocent bellman scooped up Buttons's dirty shirts, with the snuggling bush baby wrapped inside, and trundled off. Buttons was surprised to find no bush baby when he returned to his room. Another full-scale search. At last, there it was, sleeping peacefully in the laundry bin.

Bush babies at the Beverly Hills Hotel? Monkeys?

No joke. No hallucination. The Beverly Hills was not only tolerant of guests who couldn't leave their pets at home, but they almost welcomed them. For five dollars extra a night, you could bring pooch and kitty along. Of course, they had to be registered. They even got their own little guest cards, although paw prints were not required.

Elizabeth Taylor always brought her pets, ill-mannered or not. (One dog caused a flap when it used a man's leg as a fire hydrant.) Taylor once registered with nine dogs.

The old policy was a wonderful convenience for someone like Liza Minnelli when her house was being painted. She and two cats moved into the hotel to escape the fumes.

The Duke and Duchess of Windsor brought their pugs. The ugly little dogs almost caused a revolt in the kitchen when the chef discovered that the filets he was preparing painstakingly each night for the Duke and Duchess were actually intended for the dogs.

The pugs, as befitted the pets of royalty, had their own puppy-sitter when their masters stepped out for the evening.

Special puppyburgers could be ordered from room service. They were mixtures of ground beef, carrots, and peas. They went for three dollars and were supposed to be quite tasty, even if you weren't a dog.

Most pets had been welcomed at the Beverly Hills, but bear cubs never were. That didn't stop the intrepid fourteen-year-old son of the Ali Ipar of Turkey from sneaking one into his room. For several days, he kept it hidden in the bathroom, without the maids' discovering it. Finally room service became suspicious of the very odd orders it kept getting—very odd even for a fourteen-year-old boy. Room service finally thought it time to clue in the front desk. A surreptitious inspection was made. Calm was maintained. The cub was evicted.

The bear ban has now been extended to kitties and puppies. In 1977, Robert de Niro showed up with seven felines to keep him company while filming the disastrous *The Last Tycoon*.

The hotel was not too happy.

One New York publisher, never one to follow rules,

couldn't bear to be without his toy poodle, hotel policy or no.

Who would notice the little fur ball? he reasoned. He was booking a bungalow. No one would be the wiser if he smuggled Cinnamon in and out by a garden path. And no one was.

Cinnamon frolicked for several days. But fun was fun, and she grew tired of exploring the publisher's patios. There were other flowers to be smelled and new hands to be licked, and off she scampered.

Two hours of covert searching followed. At last, Cinnamon was discovered on a nearby patio, playing with some Parisian guests, who had been more than happy to puppy-sit.

It seemed quite logical, said Jennifer, a seven-year-old in the party, for a French poodle to seek out a Parisian couple.

Come check-out time, the publisher was relishing having put one over on the hotel. On the way out, a desk clerk said that it had been very nice seeing him again, adding, "And we aren't even going to mention the dog."

§   §   §   §   §   §   §   §   §   §

All hijinks and hanky-panky aren't as lighthearted as when Warren Beatty spotted director Norman Jewison as he stepped off the elevator. Jewison had just directed the Academy Award–winning *In the Heat of the Night.* Beatty, on seeing him, fell to his knees, hands prayerful.

"Please direct me. Please direct me."

He seemed to mean it.

Some carryings-on are of a darker nature.

§   §   §   §   §   §   §   §   §   §

Phil Spector, a rock producer known for his "Wall of Sound" backgrounds and his cameo as a drug dealer in

Easy Rider, had decided to have a nightcap in the Polo Lounge.

His car weaving up the porte cochere made the car jockeys think that a drink was the last thing Mr. Spector needed on top of what he must have been ingesting earlier.

A while later, out came Spector to retrieve his car. As he was waiting, another couple, middle-aged, sedate, came out of the hotel in search of their car.

There they waited. Spector, with his white-dyed, electrified-Brillo-pad hairdo, looking spaced-out and spacey. And the couple, Brooks Brothers, Peck & Peck proper.

The gentleman in the couple made a *bon mot* that Spector couldn't hear and if he had, wouldn't have been able to decipher. The lady laughed.

Spector was insulted, deciding she was laughing at him.

This was an insult. He did the only thing possible under the circumstances. He lunged for Peck & Peck's throat. As the car jockeys looked on, dumbfounded, the gentleman attempted to extricate his companion from Spector's stranglehold.

Spector is a slip of a fellow. He must have decided the odds weren't to his liking. So he did the only thing possible under the circumstances. He pulled a gun.

There he stood waving the thing around as if he had overdosed on John Wayne movies, screaming and yelling, until the Beverly Hills police arrived to disarm him.

Phil Spector, gold records and all, was no longer welcome at the Beverly Hills Hotel.

§   §   §   §   §   §   §   §   §   §

Another less than decorous, though not so dramatic display under the porte cochere:

Vanessa Redgrave, very pregnant with Franco Nero's child, came weaving out with him on the way to the shiny red Cadillac convertible that Universal Studios had thoughtfully provided. Problem was, they were so stoned that their path kept taking them off the red carpet into the flower beds, even though the entrance walk was almost fifteen feet wide.

When the shiny red Cadillac was brought up for them, Redgrave got behind the wheel. Laughing hilariously, she managed to hit the convertible button so the top kept going up and down while she pushed the ignition until the engine caught fire.

It was a display the hotel was less than happy with.

At least Redgrave never chased maids down the hallway with a broom.

Judy Garland did. Her fits were so notorious that once when her name appeared on the guest list alerting the various departments whom to expect, three-quarters of the maids called in sick.

§ § § § § § § § § §

Dopers are often no more difficult to deal with than over-indulgers in alcohol. Sometimes knowing how to prevent scenes is a matter of experience.

There have always been hard drinkers at the Beverly Hills. If industrialist Peter Fairchild staggers out from the Polo Lounge and needs help getting his Bentley to Bel-Air, the hotel knows what to do.

(Of course, those staff members available for the duty would flip a coin to see who the unlucky driver would be. For although the tip was good, it was an unpleasant assignment.

(For years Mrs. Fairchild never appeared at the hotel. Some of the night crew even suggested she was a myth. The myth, however, appeared one night in search of the Mr.

(If Mr. was a tippler, Mrs. was a guzzler. She was gone, blotto.

(She managed the two steps up from the driveway before falling on her face. The car jockeys were marshaled into carrying her into an empty room—quickly.

(The Mrs. was out through it all. No one heard any reaction when she awoke the next morning in an unfamiliar room—but then again, no one was totally certain she did awaken.

(Her maid showed up quite early and got her back to the sanctuary of Bel Air.

(While all this took place, the Mr. was in the Polo Lounge as was his custom. If he had wanted to look in on his beloved sleeping it off in a luckily available room, he wouldn't have been able to, since making it to the elevator and up to the room unassisted was quite beyond his capabilities by that late in the day. Over the years he had perfected his routine—up from the table, through the lobby, out to the car, then let the good angels drive him home.

(Deviation was impossible.)

Drugs and dope cause shudders at the Beverly Hills. Even when those indulging are pampered children of the established rich and powerful.

Ms. Susan checked in with a friend dubbed Olive Oyl because of her resemblance to Popeye's girlfriend.

Though Olive's antecedents were unknown, Susan came from money.

Susan and Olive were given a suite suitable to the standing of Susan's family in America. It didn't suit Susan and Olive, however. The rooms weren't right. Too ordinary, too conventional. They needed life, color; they needed red lightbulbs. And the lampshades. So unoriginal. They got turned upside-down. So the effect wouldn't be spoiled by distractions, Susan and Olive hung up towels over the windows to block out outside light.

Maude the Maid was appalled. She reported the redecorations to the front desk.

Susan's bizarre taste might have been overlooked by the management, except that she chose to compound her strangeness by inviting a lot of queerly dressed friends to go swimming in the pool. They wore nothing but flowers.

Multimillion inheritance or no, nude dipping is forbidden, with no exception. The police arrived to clear the pool and clear out Susan and Olive.

In helping the women pack, the police found enough marijuana to warrant arresting the heiress, and off the duo went.

The unpleasant incident was closed, or should have been. Except for Susan.

She had somehow crashed far enough to talk not only her way, but Olive's, out of jail, claiming she'd been framed. A friend must have left the noxious weed in her room, she said. Out of the pokey, Susan performed her second miracle.

She got back into the hotel.

It must have been a case of one shift not knowing what the other was doing. By the time the two shifts had coordinated enough to know that Susan and Olive had to be asked not to darken the porte cochere any more, the women had been into some serious drugging.

No floating down, no crashing, no sleeping it off—the women were ordered out, immediately.

You might say that Olive and Susan were being marched out through the lobby, but that would be completely ignoring their non-state of being. They were being escorted out, and good riddance, except that at that moment, Olive went clunko.

Bang she was out, onto the floor, and there was no reviving her. The in-house nurse, Margaret Berg, arrived almost instantaneously. Olive was dragged into the back office.

"She's had a heart attack," was Margaret Berg's diagnosis. "Hand me the amyl nitrate."

The nurse hurriedly and anxiously waved the stimulant under Olive's nose to revive her.

Olive's eyes fluttered. She was awakening, moaning orgasmically, "More, more, more! Ohhhh, ah, I lo-ah-ve all of you. . . ."

It took no advanced degree in nursing to tell those crowded into the room that Olive was no heart-attack victim.

"Get this girl out of here," sputtered a hotel executive. "All she needs is some drying out."

So ended Olive and Susan at the Beverly Hills Hotel.

§   §   §   §   §   §   §   §   §   §

By contrast, it was relatively easy merely to put a guard at the men's room door whenever a drunk Laurence Harvey went in. From experience, the staff knew that any good-looking male faced attack if he was unfortunate enough to be in there when Harvey was on the prowl. Directing men to some other men's room was surely much easier than having a disturbance and calling the cops.

At almost any hotel, police are a last resort. Things occur at a hotel that are beyond a management's control, that the hotel is in no way responsible for. But let a hotel get adverse publicity and the stigmatized establishment may suffer from a drop in bookings.

(It doesn't seem to be the fault of the Bellevue Stratford in Philadelphia that American Legion conventioneers happened to be hit with the Legionnaire's disease while there. As it turns out the disease, with its plague-like properties, has been striking here and there for years. But that's little comfort to the Bellevue Stratford. Not only did guests no longer want to stay there overnight, but local lunch and dinner patrons no longer thought it healthy or wise to dine there. Close the doors on one hotel.)

But there are occasions, even at the most closed-mouthed establishment, when the police have to be called.

§   §   §   §   §   §   §   §   §   §

Some would argue convincingly that Bill, and not

George, was blessed with the looks in the Hamilton family. While George chose to keep off the unemployment lines by starring in *Evel Knievel* and *Doctor, You've Got to Be Kidding,* Bill contributed to art through his interior decorating.

Both were widely known around the hotel. George picked up Lynda Bird Johnson, in a rented Rolls, when they went on their Academy Awards date.

It was Bill, however, who stumbled into the lobby one night through a garden entrance. If he had not been such a regular, those manning the front desk might not have recognized him. He was bruised and bloodied, clothes in shreds—in short, beaten to a Dashiell Hammett pulp.

There was no question that the police had to be called. When they arrived they managed to extract from the sorrowful Bill an equally sorrowful tale.

Bill had been driving that ignoble section of Sunset Boulevard known as the Strip. There, he saw two young fellows thumbing a ride. Being of good heart, Bill stopped for them. They, being of not so good heart, showed their appreciation by beating him up and taking his car.

The desk clerks questioned Bill's sanity. The cop taking notes said nothing until after George had retrieved his brother and left.

The note-taking cop shook his head.

"Well," he said, shredding the report, "we know what *that* was all about."

§   §   §   §   §   §   §   §   §   §

No hotel needs that publicity. If there are to be carryings-on, let them be carefree and Count Simonelli.

The count's tale begins as far away from the Beverly Hills Hotel as anything can begin.

It begins in the office of the comptroller of the City of New York. Count—but no that comes later—Mr. Peter Simonelli, hardworking civil servant, worked in that office. And it is time for his vacation.

The story of what transformed Peter Simonelli, hard-working civil servant, into hardliving bon vivant Count Simonelli, was told in Bill Davidson's *The Real and the Unreal*, the chapter called "Peter, Peter, Lotus Eater." And apparently it is all true.

So there's Peter, and about the only thing that set apart this sixtyish, white-haired chap from his fellow civil servants was that he had accrued a six-week vacation and he had an eager-beaver nephew who had become a hotshot executive at a Hollywood movie studio.

As long as he's going on vacation, why not visit Nephew Charlie?

"I thought maybe I'd drop in to see you," Pete said.

"Drop in to see me, hell," Charlie said. "If you're going to be here you'll stay with me as my guest in my suite at the Beverly Hills Hotel for a week, ten days, as long as you want."

So Charlie got on his bus, made some intermittent stops, and arrived in downtown Hollywood, where he asked his driver the easiest way to get to the Beverly Hills Hotel.

The bus driver gave him the once-, and then the twice-over and said, "You must be mixed up. That hotel isn't on our route."

Pete took a cab.

The hotel wasn't exactly what he was used to. Pete got in a struggle with the bellman who tried to relieve him of his knapsack, which was filled with sandwiches. He liked his suite, although he thought he'd have to share it, it was so big.

The first night Charlie took him to a party at Ciro's, where Pete mingled with James Stewart, Van Heflin, and Janet Leigh.

At breakfast, Pete was all ready to go out to a diner, when Charlie explained that at the Beverly Hills food was brought to the room—on a table with all the dishes with silver covers, and vases of flowers, and a large sheet of pink cellophane over the whole shebang.

Is it breakfast or lunch, and what does it cost? Pete wanted to know.

Six dollars. (This was several years ago.)

"What!" exclaimed Pete. "Six dollars for two eggs, a couple of pieces of lousy bacon, and toast? What are they charging you for, the silver?"

Charlie had to leave Pete at the swimming pool, but he sent over his girlfriend Betty to keep him company. Only thing was, Pete was no longer sitting in the sand. And he wasn't in the hotel.

At 6:15, Pete showed up.

"Where have you been?" Charlie wanted to know.

"Oh," said Pete, "Ann Blyth called you, and I got to talking to her on the phone, and she asked me to come over to have a drink with her and her Uncle Pat. So her uncle came to pick me up, and I went over to see them."

But that wasn't all.

"We're all having dinner with Ann Blyth at the Cock and Bull," where Ann gave Uncle Pete a great big kiss and spent the evening chattering away with Betty and Pete while Charlie, bemused, sat ignored.

The next morning Betty calls—for Pete, not Charlie. Charlie is able to go to work knowing Pete will be in lovely hands.

To double check—Charlie kept having visions of a lonely old man, sitting in the sand trying to imagine he was at the Coney Island beach—he called the hotel again at midmorning.

"Would you connect me with Room 424?" Charlie asked the hotel operator.

"Oh, Mr. Simonelli is at the pool."

Pete, it would seem, had caught on to leaving messages as to whereabouts. No one likes to miss a call in Hollywood—who knows what deal will be waiting at the end of a telephone line?

"Mr. Simonelli?" the pool attendant said. "He's in cabaña 2."

A cabaña, well, Pete really was in the swing of things.
A girl answered the cabaña phone.

"Mr. Simonelli is in swimming right now. Would you like to leave a message?"

"Tell him his nephew called."

"Oh, Charlie, this is Betty. Your uncle is just *wonderful*. We had the *greatest* breakfast in his patio, and we just had planter's punches, and we're going to have lunch here in his cabaña at the pool."

On hanging up, Charlie was startled to realize that Uncle Pete had taken over. "Already he's learned to sign tabs. So it's *his* patio and *his* cabaña." And it was obviously becoming *his* girl.

At dinner that night in the Lanai Room, it was Pete and not Charlie the maitre d'hôtel greeted. "A table for three for Mr. Simonelli," although Charlie had eaten there for years.

Furthermore, it seemed as if Pete knew half the people in the dining room from his day at the pool. He nodded here, shook hands there, and managed to get a few kisses thrown in for good measure.

After dinner, Charlie turned in, but Pete headed for the Polo Lounge, whence he didn't return until after 2:00 A.M.

Three days later, Charlie is again trudging home from the studio. He stops at the pool to collect his bon-vivant uncle.

"Are you looking for Count Simonelli?" the attendant asked.

Count? The count, it seems, was entertaining on the terrace, surrounded by two actresses and a producer's daughter.

"Girls, I'd like you to meet my nephew. He's one of those working men. They let you off early today, Charlie?"

A page for the count came. Charlie took the call, and on the other end was Tony Curtis.

"Howya doin', Count?"

"Count, my ass," said Charlie. "What the hell are you doing paging my uncle and calling him Count?"

"Don't get mad," Curtis laughed. "I was just trying to help the old boy along socially by phoning a few times and asking for Count Simonelli. He didn't resist."

After that, as Davidson wrote, it was

> sheer *Alice in Wonderland.* There was a constant round of cocktail parties, luncheons and dinners. By now, Charlie's old girl friend Betty, had become Pete's steady date and official hostess, and Charlie couldn't even get her on the phone any more. In addition, Pete had a retinue of starlets and socialites surrounding him at all times. He was invited to a big party at Janet Leigh's house and told to bring a guest. Charlie was his guest. At the hotel, he was treated as if he were another Howard Hughes. One night Charlie came home late and there was a new man at the front desk. Charlie asked for the key to Suite 424 and the desk clerk said coldly, "Do you have permission to go into that room?" "Permission!" hollered Charlie. "I live there." The clerk said, "Would you wait just a moment, please?" and he disappeared into the Polo Lounge. A few seconds later he came back. "It's all right," he said to Charlie. "Count Simonelli says you may go up to his room."

Then it was over—pumpkin time returned. Pete packed up the count in his suitcase, and he was off—to the bus station.

§   §   §   §   §   §   §   §   §   §

Civil servant to royalty in three short days?

Reality gets hazy around the edges at the Pink Palace. Fantasy is easy to come by.

Chapter Ten

Money.

The lifeblood of the hotel, coursing through its every level, from the Silbersteins and Slatkins, down to the Mexican maids who clean the rooms.

A couple of dollars to the bellman. Five or twenty to the manager if you're a VIP and he "rooms" you.

A bowl of room service oatmeal: $2.10. $11.00 for the "Ground Sirloin Steak, Maison."

If it's a "No, sir—I'm sorry, there are no cabañas available today," from Svend the poolkeeper, you press a picture of your father into his palm, a Lincoln or Hamilton. Then it's "Wait one second; there might just be one at the end."

A bill to Walter for front row center in the Polo Lounge. A dollar or more for the young fellow who two-wheels your Caddy up from the parking lot. A little something for the reservations manager, for being so nice getting you the exact suite you wanted. And finally a gratuity envelope for the nice maids who tidy up in the morning, turn down your sheets at night, and make sure that you have enough thick, fuzzy towels to dry off the crew of a 747.

There's money at the Beverly Hills Hotel.

Lots of it.

Money spent. Money earned. Money tossed around with

seeming abandon. And once in a while, money obtained through some slapdash of flimflammery.

By New York standards, rooms at the hotel are not extravagantly expensive. A simple four walls, bed, and color TV at the Plaza costs between $65 and $130 a night. A lovely, soft blue room with an enormous picture window overlooking the garden of the Beverly Hills, such as room 273, costs $61.

The four-bedroom penthouse suite at the New York Hilton will put the indulger in luxury back $981 a night. Bungalow 2 at the Beverly Hills, the one Norton Simon enjoyed while courting Jennifer Jones, costs $170 with two bedrooms and $284 with four. Bungalow 1, with its two bedrooms, costs $200. (Gore Vidal's mother lived in 1 for years. He passed his furloughs at the hotel during World War II.)

Bungalow 5, the favorite of Queen Juliana, the Shah of Iran (he occupied it with both Soraya and her predecessor, Empress Farah), and Princess Grace commands $195 a night with two bedrooms, $340 with five.

You don't get a "deal" at the Beverly Hills. Stay one night or one year, you still are charged the same daily rate. The average stay is three nights, although there are three year-round guests—George Barrie of Faberge, NBC's Dave Tebet, and Miss Ruth Prell. They all pay the daily rate.

The hotel exudes money. The atmosphere is heavy with it. From the piles of Vuitton luggage in the lobby to the mountains of cracked crab and lobster being wheeled by on a serving cart, here, obviously, is a place where people with money gather.

No one else could afford it.

(At times, even wealthy people wonder if the hotel is affordable. Advertising executive Mary Wells Lawrence— remember the "end of the plain plane" campaign?—asked that a hairbrush be sent up from the drugstore and billed to her room. There were several gulps and a loss of breath when she noticed that the ordinary-looking brush was taking a thirty-six-dollar chunk out of her pocketbook.)

It's not hard to spend money at the Beverly Hills. There are so many good things and good ways to spend it. Norton Simon in his year-long stay managed to slither his bill up to more than seventy thousand dollars.

Adnan Khashoggi, the Arab entrepreneur deemed "mysterious" by the *New York Times*, easily spent fifty thousand dollars in three months. A cousin of Saudia Arabian King Faisal replenished his supply of money while he was sick with a liver ailment by having his embassy deliver packages of cash, neatly wrapped in brown paper, to the front desk. Elizabeth Taylor spent more than twenty thousand dollars in two weeks during one of her visits with Richard Burton. (Of course, 20th Century-Fox was picking up the tab.)

Money central is the accounting office, a warren of nooks and offices in what used to be the garden teahouse. In it a staff of approximately a dozen runs the credit checks, totals and tallies, and handles billing.

A little more than a year and a half ago, the hotel changed a major money policy.

It had been running more than $2.5 million in house accounts—a total that made the management queasy. To get bills down to a more reasonable level—about $1 million now—the hotel began asking all guests for a major credit card. An imprint is made of that to assure the hotel of payment.

It used to be that once a credit check was run—and one is run on almost every new guest—and a reservation accepted, checking in meant signing your name at the desk. If your stay was a long one, the hotel presented a bill once a week.

Now every morning finds the credit manager scrutinizing all charges made the day before to keep tabs on high bills. It's easy to run up a tab—a business chat over a couple of rounds of tall drinks in the Polo Lounge can be ten or fifteen dollars; breakfast in the coffee shop, four or five dollars; dinner in the new restaurant, The Coterie, thirty or forty dollars; lunch at the pool, twenty or thirty dollars. Within a few days your bill can edge past the Gross National Product.

Cleveland Amory once chided *U.S. News and World Report* for omitting the Beverly Hills from a list of America's grand hotels.

"Where else," he wondered, "can the jaded traveler order a glass of orange juice in a coffee shop, having to pay for it what would be a mere couple of nights at a chain hotel? And where else could you complain of this, as I did one morning to the chef and have my furious 'This is the most expensive coffee shop in the world' met with only a slightly raised-eyebrow reply, 'I should hope so, sir'?"

Rod Steiger, staying at the hotel compliments of a movie studio, had been installed in a tiny forty-five-dollar-a-night room. The studio wouldn't ante up for anything more commodious. Steiger was furious at this less-than-big-star treatment. For revenge, he and his chauffeur dined nightly in the Maisonette Room, easily eating more than two hundred dollars' worth a sitting. The studio had neglected to put a ceiling on Steiger's food bill.

When the credit manager spots a bill blasting off, cash is requested on account, despite the credit-card imprint. Depending on what sweet somethings a bank has whispered to the accounting office, a guest's credit limit usually runs between one thousand and five thousand dollars.

Like any other business dealing with credit, the hotel has had its share of deadbeats, wretches banished forever to the hotel's blacklist. Slow payers, check bouncers, no payers make the list. Ernie Kovacs had a place of honor on it.

Woe be to any clerk who neglects to check the blacklist—there are about five hundred names on it—when checking in a new guest. One clerk got snookered when he didn't check the list *and* skipped the important credit-card imprint. The guest was able to champagne and caviar his bill to more than sixteen hundred dollars before he slipped out a side entrance, never to be seen again. The clerk was fired immediately but managed to get hired the same day at the Beverly Wilshire.

Some bill skippers have blithely sashayed through the lobby on their way out—with bellmen toting their luggage.

Byron Moger had been the vice-president of Manufacturers Trust in New York and then executive vice-president of another large bank chain before retiring to live the good life and to drink his way to happiness.

The alcohol and high living soon depleted Moger's resources—monetary and physical. All his credit cards had run out or been revoked—all save one. He still had a house account at the Beverly Hills Hotel.

It was Santa Claus season when Moger checked in and started ordering champagne and chateaubriand. His bill got bigger and bigger, with no cautionary word from the accounting office, but Moger knew that sooner or later the hotel would catch on to his destitution.

Christmas Eve. On January 1 the premium would be due on his life insurance for his two sons. Moger knew there was no way he could pay it, but he wanted his sons to have something.

That night, with the help of many pills and lots of whiskey, Moger committed suicide.

Naturally, in the annals of the Beverly Hills, suicides aren't mentioned. If you ask about Byron Moger, you will receive a completely blank look.

§   §   §   §   §   §   §   §   §   §

Although there is money to be made at the hotel, employees don't make it in straight salary. Working the desk for fifteen years translates into eight hundred dollars a month.

In addition, there is no job security, despite a house union. A longtime employee can be dismissed on a moment's notice: "We don't want you here and goodbye."

So why do so many employees stick around for ten, fifteen, thirty years?

Tips.

Khashoggi tossing away five hundred dollars. Liz Taylor tipping her maid fifty dollars. A stocks-and-bonds purveyor who had hung out in bungalow 10 for three months, presenting everyone he dealt with at the hotel fifty dollars each at Christmas.

Some of the most appreciative gifts come from happy guests who were given "their" rooms. All the rooms at the hotel are nice; it's just that some are nicer than others.

And they are in demand.

There are some people who would kill—or part with a twenty or a hundred-dollar bill—to be able to say, "Oh yes, drop by. I'm in bungalow 5." And when these people get that bungalow, they like to show their gratitude to the clerk or manager responsible.

Which leads to the great rack wars.

The Alsace-Lorraine of the Beverly Hills, the rack is merely a slot setup showing all the rooms of the hotel and who is going to occupy them. When a specific room is wanted, that slot will be blocked off, indicating the room is not to be assigned to anyone else.

Often guests will deal with a one person at the hotel. They know that Hollis Polodna will ensure that they get suite 486, with its fireplace and king-size bed—Johnny Carson's old favorite. Or 483–484, the suite favored by Joseph Levine.

Once one of the assigners wangles a room for his guest, the room-rack slot gets a yellow block meaning hands off or a red block meaning *absolutely* hands off. If a Polodna guest happens to be showing up at the same time as a Brown guest and both want the same room, it hasn't been unknown for names to be lifted from the rack and substituted.

War ensues.

Polodna, Brown, Bill Bixby, and Nick Pappas are the principal room assigners, although Slatkin and Silberstein make a few from time to time.

It's all subjective, but some rooms are just considered better than others. In the main building, the super-desirable ones are those facing the garden, and of those most are in the newer Crescent Wing. (Rooms in the front get street noise.) 486, at $215 a night, is the biggest suite, with an enormous sitting room, although 483–484, at $165, is cozier.

Of the bungalows, 5, fronting on Crescent Drive, with its four bedrooms, is the largest. It also has its own kitchen, dining room, patio, and terrace. Dave Tebet of NBC favors this one.

But big isn't necessarily best.

Bungalows 6, 8, and 9 are highest on the status scale. Record-company millionaire Ahmet Ertegun usually opts for 8, as does Dirk Bogarde. (On one trip Bogarde was staying with his male traveling companion and being sent vases and vases of flowers. However, the staff had to be warned—and it was noted on his preference card—that no flowers should be accepted from Glynis Johns. Johns, it seems, had been married at one time to Bogarde's companion, and Dirk was a very jealous type.)

Bungalow 9, which on occasion has housed Jackie Gleason, Tony Bennett, and Perry Como, is actually a duplex that can be split into two separate rentals. It has two living rooms with bars, five bedrooms, powder rooms for visitors, two kitchens, and five baths. All for only $565—or you can chintzy it and take just one bedroom and living room for $165.

Bungalow 7 (two bedrooms at $185, all four for $111 more) was the choice of Yves Montand and Simone Signoret when he was in town to co-star with Barbra Streisand in *On a Clear Day You Can See Forever.* The desk kept getting complaints from neighbors when Montand would repair to the porch to practice his songs.

In bungalow 3 ($190 for two bedrooms, $373 for all five) Ernie Brown told Robert Kennedy's children of their father's assassination and then stayed with them and their Occidental College baby-sitter until the doctor came.

It was in bungalow 12 (now going for $155 for two bedrooms, $202 for three) that a Mr. Keck lived for three years. Mr. Keck was into oil and could afford the bungalow that had increased in price from the ninety-some-odd dollars a day he had originally paid for it. Mr. Keck moved out, however, when one Christmas, as a holiday cheer, the management had a gift plant put on his porch. Unfortunately the plant wilted before Mr. Keck received it, and his name had been misspelled on the card.

The "bad"—only by comparison—bungalows are 14 to 21, which are actually bungalow suites in a two-story building. They are near the laundry and garage and therefore noisy. In the main building, Siberia is rooms facing Sunset and most especially rooms near elevators. Noise.

It's a game of status points, who gets which rooms, just as, Svend complains, certain lounges at the pool are the place to sun.

Guest gratitude doesn't necessarily take the form of cash. One bellman and his wife were flown down to a New Year's Eve party in Texas by an appreciative guest.

And of course, not everyone tips.

Rosalind Russell and her husband, Freddie Brisson, didn't tip the car jockeys. Which was why Rosalind Russell and husband always had to wait fifteen minutes for their car.

David Frost is another congenital stiffer. He's consistent, though, tipping no one. After one trip, he was annoyed with what he felt were a lot of outstretched hands. So he sent a letter to Silberstein explaining that although he had a no-tipping policy, the service had been so mah-velous that he was enclosing a quarter to be split among the employees.

Silberstein was not amused. In fact, he was so un-amused that he wanted to send a scathing reply. The more level-headed Muriel intervened, reminding her father that a snide remark or two by Frost on his television show would not be the kind of publicity the hotel needed or deserved.

The matter was dropped. Frost still doesn't tip.

§   §   §   §   §   §   §   §   §   §

There aren't many like Frost. Tips make for an enviable bank balance. But there are temptations to supplement even that. Temptations to skim a little, flim a little, flam a little.

Certainly with a staff the size of the Beverly Hills, there is going to be a little fudging, some gouging, and a touch of downright dishonesty once in a while. There's too much easy-prey money floating around for there not to be.

What must that maid have thought, the maid making a minimum wage, when she pushed her cleaning cart to suite 486 after the guests had checked out? Even if the maid hadn't known who the guests were, she would have known they were top-drawer, four aces, VIPs. After all, the suite had been redecorated just for them. They had been Princess Margaret and Lord Snowdon, and they had left minutes before.

While dusting the maid found a case on the desk. Curious, she opened it. Inside were Princess Margaret's assortment of jewelry, which she had neglected to take.

That maid was honest, but there was a clerk who happened to forget to tell an advertising executive that a package of jewels had arrived for his magazine layout. Not only did the clerk forget, but he also took the jewels home with him. The process of elimination led the cops to his door, and the fellow not only lost his job, but got sent to the pokey.

Another employee was nabbed in 1960 for embezzling thirty-six thousand dollars over six years. Bookkeeper Elizabeth Hebard, described as a mild-mannered spinster, made out paychecks for nonexistent employees.

When arrested—she was watering the African violets—Hebard muttered, "I knew they would find out sooner or later."

Some employees have added to their take-home pay in somewhat less larcenous ways.

Roses, for instance.

A guest will often bring a request to the front desk that a dozen long-stems be sent to a girlfriend, a mother, or a wife.

"Put it on my bill," the guest will say.

Now, a dozen roses from the hotel flower shop could easily cost thirty-five to forty dollars. If the clerk gets the roses there. But more enterprising ones have been known to slip out to a cheapie florist, pick up the same flowers for fifteen or twenty dollars, wrap them up in some dime-store paper, and have them delivered. The guest will still find a thirty-five- or forty-dollar charge on his bill, but the enterprising clerk will have made himself an easy twenty dollars.

Tickets, for instance.

Say Dino de Laurentiis is checking in. His impending arrival will be mentioned in the trade papers. Studios and fellow producers will send over complimentary tickets to movie premieres or shows down at the Music Center. Or a Clive Davis of Arista Records will get freebies for the sold-out Rolling Stones or Elton John concert.

The tickets arrive at the desk. The intended recipients, however, have no idea they've been sent. A clerk will sometimes sell the tickets to another guest who really would love to be blasted into the next county by Mick Jagger.

Bellmen pick up extra money by keeping their own supply of liquor to be sold after hours to thirsty guests. The markup, not unexpectedly, is stupendous. Even so, once in a while, someone who received no liquor might have a charge on his bill nonetheless. Some Arabs, teetotalers all, got cozened with a four-hundred-dollar liquor charge, which they never noticed.

Johnny Carson's bill was padded every so often when he was going through his drinking period. He'd get so smashed that he wouldn't be able to remember the next morning whether he had made any charges the night before.

Bill padding is a fact of any hotel's life, no matter what safeguards management tries to erect.

Some people offer too much of an easy target.

Elizabeth Taylor is one. She is someone who buys fourteen hundred dollars' worth of panty hose at a Beverly Hills store and instructs that the cost be added to her hotel bill.

Twentieth Century-Fox happened to be picking up her bill while she was finishing *The Only Game in Town*, a Las Vegas picture filmed in Paris and Hollywood.

On that twenty-thousand-dollar visit, Taylor was hit with a two-thousand-dollar charge for "postage and packages," when she hadn't sent a single postcard.

Clerks keep supplies of their own stamps. When a guest wants something mailed, the clerk stamps it and submits a chit—a paid-out slip—to the cashier, who then reimburses him with cash. The charge is then entered on the guest's tab.

In the case of Taylor, some wily person or persons assumed that she wouldn't deign to line-read the bill and that no one at 20th would have the nerve to question her.

20th had to shrug off a lot of Taylor expenses on that film. For one thing, her character wore rings on every finger in the movie, rings costing a couple of thousand dollars each, from David Webb in New York. After shooting, it slipped Taylor's mind to return them to props.

It wasn't the last time she suffered from forgetfulness. In

a later film, *Zee and Co.*, she raved to the wardrobe girl about a silk blouse she had to wear. "Would you get me the same blouse in twelve other shades?" Taylor requested.

The wardrobe girl did. She was very distressed later when she went to retrieve them, and Taylor informed her that "Oh, I made a mistake and packed them all. They must be in Switzerland by now."

The girl, fearing she'd have to pay for the blouses, since they had been her responsibility, went to the film's producer.

"Forget it," he told her. "On the last film Taylor cost the production thirty thousand dollars in jewelry. At least this time all she wanted was some silk shirts."

§ § § § § § § § § §

Another ploy used for padding a bill is merely submitting a paid-out with a scrawled forgery. Often a husband and wife—this happened to the Joseph Levines—don't know what the other is signing and assume charges are legitimate.

"You'd be surprised," an employee remarked, "how many married couples don't speak to each other." Padding and bill doctoring don't happen often, and the management cringes at the notion they occur at all. Nonetheless, padding is a hazard of hotelling. Anyone might be the victim.

Anyone except Ethel Merman. It doesn't matter who's paying her bill. It could be Ethel herself or NBC playing host when she appears on *The Tonight Show*. There are never any mistakes on Merman's bill.

She ensures that.

It's her ritual. Whenever she returns to the hotel in the evening or night, Merman asks to see her bill for the day's charges.

Invariably, after a moment of squinting, she says, "I

can't read it here. I'll take it to my room and bring it back to you."

Set your watches. On your mark. In five minutes, without fail, the front-desk phone is ringing.

"What the fuck is this twelve cents on my bill? I haven't been here all day. I haven't even made a phone call. Get down to my room, get this bill, and have this taken off. Then bring the goddamn thing back so I can check it."

Every day. Without fail.

Then the clerks have to go through every charge made in the hotel looking for Merman's twelve-center. Two hours later they find it. Usually she has forgotten that she stopped in the drugstore or had a bite in the coffee shop. Once the evidence is produced, Merman is happy.

Until the next night.

§ § § § § § § § § §

Flimflam danger also comes from outside talent.

The hotel can do a certain amount to curb employee mischief. Harder to combat are out-and-out, straightforward robberies, occurrences the hotel doesn't like to discuss.

There have been major ones that had to make the papers, usually because they took place in the lobby. In 1936 Gilbert Roland got himself a walk-on in a holdup.

Two bandits entered and herded everyone in sight, including Roland, into the auditor's office.

A switchboard operator got a call through to the police just as one bandit spotted her.

"Take off that headset," he ordered.

When she didn't comply fast enough, the bad guy ripped it from her head. The operator later told reporters that "Roland started forward, but the bandit turned his gun on him."

They got away with thirteen hundred dollars.

In 1943 four "youthful" holdup men scurried off with

bags filled with money and jewelry, but they got only a few blocks away before the police started showering them with bullets.

These were straight-out, hands-up-in-the-lobby robberies. Call the cops and let them deal with it. They are not serious impingements on a hotel's reputation. Much easier to acknowledge than the problem with bungalow 9. It kept being robbed, right after it was redecorated.

One widow of a television executive was robbed twice, once for a couple of hundred thousand dollars in jewelry. It didn't make her switch hotels, but she did take to making frightened calls in the middle of the night claiming someone was trying to jimmy her door.

There are robberies at the hotel, but for reputation's sake, they are often hushed up.

Outside talent also go in for impersonations. Usually all this consists of is getting a look at the guest list that is sent to all departments. The lists are distributed so that, say, a waiter in the Coterie will know that so and so is in room such and such and that name and that room should appear together on the check when it is signed.

An impersonator will sneak a peek at the list and start signing someone else's name.

There are always variations, however.

Take the time a reservation was made for Orson Welles, a frequent guest of the hotel.

Come the appointed day, and sure enough, there is Welles, looking unusually fit and healthy. The clerks even compliment him effusively on losing so much weight. "Mr. Welles, we've never seen you looking so well."

It is good to see that Mr. Welles (usually a dead ringer for the Goodyear blimp) has shed a few pounds.

Off Welles goes to his bungalow, bags being toted by Alberto, the bellman.

A few minutes later, Alberto, now a disturbed bellman, returns to the lobby.

"You know, there's something wrong. I don't believe that is Orson Welles."

"What are you talking about, Alberto? We all know Orson Welles as well as you do, and that's who it is."

"No, there's something funny."

Alberto was not to be shaken. He was positive. He had carried Welles's luggage too many times over too many miles for too many years not to know his man.

But how as he going to convince everyone else?

Then he had it.

Alberto went to the kitchen and prevailed upon the room-service operator to put through a call to the Welles bungalow.

"Mr. Welles, would you like to order breakfast now? If you tell me what time you'd like it delivered, you can have it first thing on waking up."

Sounded good to Welles, so he placed his order.

With that, Alberto had all the proof he needed.

It seems that the real Orson Welles eats the same breakfast every morning.

This "Orson Welles" had ordered something different.

§   §   §   §   §   §   §   §   §   §

Helft's clothing and accessories, the beauty shop, the barber, parking, the valet—none are owned by the hotel. They are concessions, space rented from the hotel.

And they are lucrative.

Smitty of the parking lot not only has his own accountant, but he was elected president of his country club.

The former owner of the valet service retired a millionaire. Some of the beauticians at the beauty shop, such as Nora, have been at the shop for more than twenty years. The money is too good to walk away from.

Nora did leave the Beverly Hills for the Beverly Wilshire. She came home quickly.

"Maybe I'm a snob," she says between curling and crimping, "but I didn't like the class of people over there."

The women at the Beverly Hills' Sunkist-orange-and-pale-yellow salon are primarily local matrons. Only 35 percent of the shop's patrons are hotel guests. But the locals keep the place filled as they get manicures, pedicures, their hair dyed the same shade of California blonde, and have the curve of their eyebrows artfully changed while sitting next to Raquel Welch, Suzanne Pleshette, and agent Sue Mengers. Fanny Brice was prettified at the Beverly Hills when she was alive.

Howard Hughes, Mike Todd, and the Duke of Windsor were barbershop regulars when they were in town. Hughes later insisted on his "no-touch" clips, which had to be done in his rooms.

Helft's, the clothing and potpourri store, has one shop in the lobby and two in the arcade. The lobby shop has a kaleidoscopic tumble of belts, boas, luggage, jewelry, peignoirs, fur coats, and other expensive trifles and trinkets.

One downstairs shop specializes in sportswear, the other in European designer clothes.

In the sixties, when her daughter was still half of the quickly forgettable Anthony and Cleopatra, Cher's mother, Georgette, worked in Helft's. She was always lamenting that her daughter had hooked up with a good-for-nothing weirdo truck driver and wouldn't someone, please, take her out on a normal date?

Helft's could be a nice place to work for someone like Georgette. It was, after all, a nice place to meet wealthy men who ate at nice places and who might once in a while drop a bauble or two onto a poor working girl.

One of the Helft's women was bubbling on Christmas morning. "Look, look, look!" she said to the desk clerks. "Look at what Jack Warner has given me!"

The present was an exquisite little necklace, sparkling with lots of little diamonds.

Then there's the parking concession, touted by the locals as being the best car valet in Los Angeles, which probably makes it the best in the country.

Your entrance puts you in a mood for the hotel. The soft curve up from mansion-strewn Sunset Boulevard arcs through semitropical bushes and under the majestic palm trees, past Mercedes, Maseratis, and Rolls, up to the stretched-out porte cochere, with its three bays for cars and all those hustling, uniformed parking attendants.

It's not hard to "make an entrance" at the Beverly Hills, as with an unconscious nudge to the accelerator you want to Errol Flynn it, Carole Lombard it up the driveway, with a flash and a squeal and a toss of the head, imagining yourself in a convertible, top down, hair blowing, handsome, beautiful, debonair, glamorous, very, very MGM.

There is no parking charge at the hotel whether you're a guest or there to pick up a copy of the *Wall Street Journal*. The only payment is the tip to the car jockey who gets your car.

It is reported that the jockey does not get to keep his tip. It all goes back to Smitty, who pays his four full-time and twenty-one student part-time employees straight salaries.

At least one car jockey, bridling at having to turn over his gratuities, stuffed part of them in a hole in a tree to be retrieved after work.

Smitty, a six-foot, four-inch man—he has found the celebrities, the Bogarts, Gables, Barrymores, Newmans "all shorter than I expected"—also provides limousine service for guests if they request it.

Smitty leases Cadillacs from a local agency and then rents them on a daily basis to guests. He can also provide a driver, if desired.

One of Smitty's services has the local cab drivers fuming. He will provide limousine service to the airport for guests. This means that the cab drivers lose the good, long fares. A side effect is that the cabs are now very slow to come when the hotel calls them. The Beverly Hills is not one of their favorite pickup spots.

§   §   §   §   §   §   §   §   §   §

There is no question that the hotel is a money maker. Slatkin says that 1977 was its best year yet, running a 98 percent occupancy year round. A figure almost unheard of for a transient hotel.

But the money, he says, goes back into the hotel.

"My family has money without the profits of the hotel."

(The family has among its holdings, property in Jamaica and La Quinta, properties for development in Puerta Vallarta, and Ruby's Dunes Restaurant in Palm Springs.)

There is money in the hotel, no matter what they choose to do with it. The Polo Lounge alone takes in $240,000 a year for food and $700,000 for liquor, making it "a little gold mine," according to a competing hotelman.

In 1974 the Beverly Hills Corporation bought 60 percent of Vagabond Hotel, Inc., a chain of forty-five motels (despite the company name). It's not surprising that as long as the Beverly Hills corporation was going to expand, it would choose motels. Slatkin once predicted that motels would become the predominant type of "inns."

"Costs are very real in the industry today," he said, "and that's one reason why the motel is doing so well. Both its construction cost and maintenance are lower, which gives it a lower cost per room. And the hotel industry is starting to fulfill the needs of the modern traveling public by giving it motels."

But he was quick to add that he felt the Beverly Hills Hotel was immune to the motel trend.

"We feel there will always be enough people in the world—and we are an international hotel—who will prefer the smaller, more compact hotel. We're elegant but very informal in many ways, and there are enough people who are willing to pay for our type of operation."

Chapter Eleven

Miss Prell was headed for her twice-weekly walk to the post office.

One step, two. She sidled down the staircase, her back pressed to the wall.

The Hertz girls saw her coming and, as usual, tried to suppress their giggles. But it was hard. Miss Prell was so . . . well, so comical, with her dyed red hair, her toreador pants and halter tops, and her bright red lipstick, which covered not only her lips, but half her gaunt face as well.

One step, two. Miss Prell had made it to the lobby floor.

The low buzz there stopped as people gawked at the apparition scuttling toward the door.

"Hello, Miss Prell," someone in the cashier's cage said, as someone in the cashier's cage invariably did.

"Oh! Oh!" answered Miss Prell as she always did.

One hour later—six blocks there, six blocks back—Miss Prell reversed her scuttle, up the stairs, back pressed to wall, a fast feint past the Hertz counter, down the hall to room 236.

Miss Prell was home safe again.

Miss Ruth Prell has been at the Beverly Hills for more than thirty years. She lives there year round and makes only three appearances a week in the lobby. Twice to go to the post office—though it has often been wondered to whom she writes—and once on Sunday to attend her Christian Science services.

Miss Prell had been on the eccentric side even when her sister, Mrs. Ethel Brown, was alive. At least then Ethel had been a bit more outgoing, so Ruth's strangeness wasn't quite as noticeable.

The two had shared a room, gone to their Christian Science meetings together, and been looked upon with good-natured tolerance. Ethel would chat with the maids once in a while, or the desk clerks, inquiring after who was in the hotel like a schoolgirl about to read *Photoplay*.

Then Ethel began feeling poorly. It was tuberculosis, but being a Christian Scientist, she didn't put herself under a doctor's care.

The maids were concerned—Mrs. Brown was so nice—but there was nothing to be done. The two sisters knew what they were about, and that was that.

One day, Ethel was worse than usual. She didn't even get out of bed when the maid came to tidy up. The cleaning was done quickly and quietly so as not to awaken her. The maid left with a nod to Miss Prell, who was sitting quietly in one of the overstuffed chairs.

"I hope Mrs. Brown is feeling better tomorrow," the maid whispered.

Ethel wasn't any better the second day. She was still in bed, eyes closed. Miss Prell was still sitting quietly in her chair.

The third day, Ethel was still asleep. While dusting, the curious maid inched over to the bed to get a better look.

"Miss Prell," she said, "I think something may be wrong. Mrs. Brown isn't moving."

"Oh yes," said Miss Prell, unperturbed. "She passed on two days ago."

Miss Prell lives alone. She makes her infrequent appearances in the lobby, and the inheritance from her family's shampoo fortune pays the bill and the gift subscriptions to the *Christian Science Monitor* she gives out to some of the hotel employees at Christmas.

§ § § § § § § § § §

Howard Hughes sidled and skulked for almost thirty years.

The Beverly Hills was one of his hidey-hole retreats.

In the 1950s and into the 60s Hughes had no fewer than four bungalows, two suites, and two rooms on a daily, year-round, no-discount basis, costing more than a thousand dollars a day.

One four-room bungalow was his. A three-room bungalow a quarter of a mile away was for his wife, Jean Peters. The third bungalow and rooms were occupied by his eight Mormon bodyguards; the suites for any guests he might have. This left the fourth bungalow. It was left empty.

No one was allowed in that bungalow, not even maintenance men. One intrepid bellboy, working on his summer vacation, did sneak a peek. What he found was inches and inches of dust sitting on piles and piles of records, engineering reports, specifications—and the blueprints for the *Spruce Goose*. The *Goose* was the transport plane, the flying boat Hughes had designed to help win World War II.

(It wasn't ready for test-flying until 1947, and then managed to get up only seventy feet and fly one short mile.)

The empty bungalow caused problems for the plumbing in all the bungalows. Since no plumbers were allowed in, the pipelines to the building eventually corroded. These lines crossed with others, and after a while all the plumbing was acting up.

Despite Hughes's various precautions to keep from being seen—he'd drive up in a panel truck that looked like a butcher's van—he was a presence at the hotel. Management never spoke of him. That was forbidden. But people were aware that he was there, nonetheless.

Nan Kirsch remembers going to the Polo Lounge with friends when she was still below the drinking age. It was fun to see whether any of the men would notice her—how could they not—and it was so sophisticated to sip on a piña colada or some other terribly grown-up drink.

Once on her way back from the ladies' room, she got turned around and started heading down an unfamiliar hallway.

Out of a shadow she hadn't even noticed, a hand shot and grabbed her shoulder.

"Miss," the owner of the hand said, "no one is allowed down this corridor. Go back the way you came."

It was spooky, just like in the movies. But she went, much faster than she had come. Safely back at her little round table in the sanctuary of the Polo Lounge she asked her waiter what the big deal was down that corridor.

"Oh," he said, lowering his voice as if he had no choice, "those are Mr. Hughes's rooms. No one goes there."

Besides his "meat" truck, Hughes kept a 1932 Chevrolet that he allowed no one else to drive. Peters would often show up in a chauffeur-driven station wagon, and there were invariably two or three cars parked around the hotel, waiting, tanks filled, for when, if ever, Hughes decided to use them.

He also kept two leased Cadillacs in the garage. They were never moved; they just sat there with their tires flat.

Year after year Hughes paid the leasing company for the privilege of the cars' disuse. He would tip the garagemen six hundred dollars at Christmas for doing nothing to keep his cars in nonworking order.

Hughes was a strange man. Mad, even. Before he became the complete recluse of later years, he would sometimes hire the orchestra in the Persian Room nightclub to play all night. He had insomnia.

Or he would slip into the Polo Lounge, for a solitary drink off in the corner, watching the conviviality of other people. According to a bellman, Hughes would also slip on his way out—into the bushes.

"Everybody was pulling Hughes out of the shrubbery—dead drunk. He'd be stoned in the garden all the time—but for the price he was paying, nobody ever said anything."

In 1951 Sheilah Graham had a strange interlude with Hughes at the hotel. Graham had the flu, but Hughes insisted that she come. He had a scoop for her. A big scoop.

As Albert B. Gerber told it in his book, *Bashful Billionaire,*

> *Ten minutes later a car arrived to pick her up. The chauffeur took her on a circuituous route which lasted more than thirty minutes. It had, by now, grown dark and Miss Graham could not identify her whereabouts any longer. Finally the car drew up at what appeared to be the back entrance of a one-story bungalow. From the shrubbery, the garbage cans and the enormous Spanish building outlined against the sky, she recognized she was at the back entrance of a Beverly Hills Hotel bungalow. Since the hotel was at most a three minute drive from her home, she concluded that the drive had been intended to confuse her.*

And the Scoop?

Howard Hughes could tell Sheilah Graham unequivocally that Elizabeth Taylor's newest gentleman friend, a high muckety-muck in the film world, was a Communist.

Graham, who had different ideas on what constituted a scoop, thanked Mr. Hughes for his information and left.

Hughes was a rabid Communist baiter. And his role in the tragedy of the Hollywood blacklistings is often overlooked.

Perhaps his fear that one of the "pinkos" he destroyed was out to get him led him to hire a food taster. For a while Hughes also had his own chef in the kitchen who did nothing but cook for him and Jean Peters. (A Hughes quirk was to call up in the middle of the night and request an upside-down cake. The Beverly Hills, being the place it was, would oblige by baking a fresh one.)

Hughes always ate in his bungalow. And Peters always ate in hers. Which didn't mean they didn't eat together. During dinner they were on the phone to each other, carrying on polite conversation as they ate.

Another Hughes idiosyncracy was the roast-beef man. This was a fellow whose entire job was to make a roast-beef sandwich, wrap it in waxed paper, and stash it in a specific tree in the garden. The man never actually saw Hughes remove the sandwich, but it was usually gone the next morning when he came with a fresh one.

When Howard abandoned the Beverly Hills for the sanctuary of Nevada, he didn't back up the vans and move out in a day. It was a gradual leavetaking. When the hotel finally got into one of his suites, it looked as if it hadn't been used in the twenty years Hughes had kept it. The decorations were exactly the same. The place was layered with dust. The draperies were crumbling off their tracks. Once he left, Hughes never came back.

§   §   §   §   §   §   §   §   §   §

Eccentrics come in all degrees at the Beverly Hills, Howard Hughes and Miss Prell at the top of the pyramid and the mildly cuckoo, with an aberration or two, at the bottom.

Diahann Carroll, in most respects and dealings with the hotel, conducts herself rationally, sensibly. She has one peculiarity. She never likes the room she is given, no matter which room it is. If her stay is a week, she will change rooms three, four, a dozen times.

"There is a little too much light in that room."

"The color of this rug hurts my eyes."

Or it might be as simple as, "I want a bigger room."

There's always a reason the room isn't right. When a new room is available maids pack up Carroll's clothes in the old room and unpack them in the new. And they pack all her cosmetics and drugs. It has been known to happen that, after one move too many, a maid will sweep off the dresser, helter-skelter into a suitcase, mixing up bottles, breaking one or two. Carroll may be fussy about rooms, but not about the damage to her cosmetics. She never complains.

Some guests have cleanliness obsessions. Marjorie Main

couldn't stand dirt, and she knew how to get rid of it. Invariably her reservations request included instructions that her room was to be thoroughly scrubbed—with Hexol, a borax-like soap that wasn't easy to find in Beverly Hills. No matter. If a prized guest wanted Hexol, the Beverly Hills made sure she got Hexol. By check-in time the room had been scrubbed and boxes of the stuff were left open around the room. Main liked the smell of it.

Novelist Jackie Susann was another clean freak. She didn't specify the products, but she did carefully list what was to be given special attention. The baseboards, the drapes, the window sills, the lightbulbs, the floor behind the toilet—hidden, often overlooked spots were to be given thorough scrubdowns.

§   §   §   §   §   §   §   §   §   §

On the other side of the dustmop are Marilyn Monroe and Elizabeth Taylor. Their rooms were so chaotic that a little dust would hardly be noticed.

Hedda Hopper, who was taking Taylor to her first party after Mike Todd's death, described the room.

"When I went in it looked as if a cyclone had hit the bedroom. Every dress she owned had been pulled out of the closets and thrown on tables, chairs, bed, or floors.

"'What shall I wear!' she was waiting as soon as I opened the door."

Hopper advised a red dress.

Taylor ran out of scattering room at one point and had a separate bungalow just for her clothes.

She could be disorganized with herself as well as her clothes. When Taylor's father died, she came west to attend his funeral and naturally stayed at the hotel.

The funeral was to begin at 11. Mrs. Taylor arrived early to fetch Elizabeth but was told that her daughter was still putting on makeup. The minutes passed and passed and passed, and it was noon, but Elizabeth had yet to make an appearance. Mrs. Taylor left.

A desk clerk seeing her leave without Elizabeth called

the bungalow to see if anything was wrong. The maid on duty answered.

"Miss Taylor will be a while yet," she explained. "She's changing her makeup. She put on one face and decided it wasn't right. So now she's doing another."

When her face was at last in place, Liz was able to depart for the mortuary.

Monroe's room was strewn with champagne and caviar and her clothes. And she was never on time. It became a daily production to transform her from what hair stylist and makeup artist George Masters called a half-crocked Hausfrau schlepping around, to the luminescent Monroe.

And people waited for it to happen.

But there was one time her studio was determined to get her somewhere on time. It was 1959. Soviet Premier Nikita Khrushchev was visiting the United States, and Monroe was scheduled to meet him.

7:00 A.M. A masseur goes to her bungalow. 9:00 A.M. Someone arrives to put on her body makeup. A third person shows up for the facial makeup. Then a stylist to arrange her baby-fine, overbleached hair.

The head of the studio, Spyros Skouras, pops in to supervise.

"She has to be there," he says.

The last item is to squeeze Monroe into a black net dress that, after a fashion, almost covers her chest.

At last, Rudi, her chauffeur, can whisk her away to the lot, five minutes away.

Marilyn Monroe was early! Through the concerted efforts of six people—a sixth had done all the arranging and orchestrating—Monroe got to the luncheon before anyone else.

And she was furious. She thought she was late and had missed the whole thing!

§   §   §   §   §   §   §   §   §   §

The nation became acquainted with Candy Mossler when

she stood trial for the murder of her husband. It was a gory, gossipy sensation that occupied headlines and conversations for weeks. When she was found not guilty, she got her freedom and a few million dollars. Husband's estate went to her, and she came to the Beverly Hills.

Candy was afraid of something. She wouldn't go into her room until a bellman checked it over.

She would stand in the lobby for a half hour as he looked in closets, under beds, behind doors. Candy was afraid someone might push her out a window, which was why she had to have a room with few windows, no balcony, and certainly nothing on the ground floor with a door leading to the garden.

§   §   §   §   §   §   §   §   §   §

It wasn't death John Lennon feared when he made arrangements for a secluded bungalow to be listed under an assumed name. It was the groupies and crazies that were hounding him and his wife, Yoko Ono.

At the Beverly Hills even groupies can be ditched.

No one paid any attention to the new guests. So many faces mill about. No alarm sounded. No crowds gathered. John and Yoko had found safe harbor, until John blew his cover. He posted four armed guards around the bungalow. That caused comments, and the groupies converged.

§   §   §   §   §   §   §   §   §   §

Orson Welles wanted to play Phantom of the Beverly Hills, so he had someone check him into bungalow 14B under an assumed name. Welles took a garden entrance, never came into the lobby, and settled with his Yugoslavian girlfriend.

People, famous people, often want their whereabouts kept secret and register incognito, but the pair in bungalow 14B was cause for discussion. The staff knew there were only two, because there were only two signatures on the room-service chits. But the room-service order was

always for three—Welles ate double portions of everything.

But before any sleuthing could be done, the incoming
calls gave him away. Rita Hayworth knew he was there.
And left messages. Friends knew he was there and left
messages. His agent, Paul Kohner, had tracked him down
and had important messages, he said. But Welles continued to accept no calls, no messages. The switchboard
notes slipped under his door went unacknowledged.

Kohner was desperate. He had to get a letter to his
client.

He offered a desk clerk ten dollars to hand deliver a note
to Welles, so at least the agent would know it had got
through.

It didn't seem like much of a task for ten dollars. It was
twilight when the clerk started banging on the door to
14B.

No answer.

Bang, bang, bang.

No answer, but the clerk was determined to get that tip.

Bang some more.

The door swings open.

There's an enormous man, totally nude, standing in the
doorway, silhouetted by a light behind him that is suddenly turned off.

"It really freaked me," the clerk said. "I opened the
screen door and said, 'There's a message for you,' and
whoosh, as fast as I could, I got out of there. The look on
his face was 'I'm going to kill you.' Man. If I'd known that
was going to happen . . . it wasn't worth ten bucks, I can
tell you."

§   §   §   §   §   §   §   §   §   §

Barbara Hutton had been a regular at the hotel ever since
she was a child coming with her bodyguard to see silent
movies.

The hotel saw her through her habits and appetites that got stranger over the years.

It got to so the Woolworth heiress would book seven rooms—one for her clothes, although she didn't wear many lying in bed all day—on the ground floor of the Crescent Wing. She didn't like maids coming in to clean. Barbara wore diamonds the size of rock candy and was in fear of being robbed. Her secretary had to hand deliver the garbage to maids waiting in the hall.

The hotel has seen her through her many husbands. One on the list would sleep in the room across the hall from his wife—kept company by a lady of the evening. The problem was, this husband had no cash. The lady had to be paid by the hotel, and the charge was added to Barbara's bill as a paid-out.

In 1975 Barbara arrived with an entourage of six. It was not a typical visit, because she had sent word ahead through her business manager that there were to be no paid-outs on the bill this time. All charges had to be okayed by the manager.

The rumor was that Barbara was overextended until another portion of her trust came due. She had become less and less extravagant with her tips. And then came the business manager's memo.

There shouldn't have been any problem with this arrangement, for in the end everyone would be taken care of. But the problem came from one of Barbara's addictions.

She was a Coca-Cola fiend. She rarely ate; she just drank Coke, by the case. These cases had to be delivered to her room. Case after case.

It took about two weeks of hauling the Coke to Barbara's room for the bellmen to decide a job action was in order.

No tips, no Cokes. Barbara's supply was cut off.

Withdrawal symptoms had her frantically on the phone with her lawyers. This was serious. She couldn't understand why she couldn't get service at the Beverly Hills Hotel.

The lawyer showed up at the bellmen's room.

"What has happened?" the lawyer asked. "Why aren't deliveries being made to Miss Hutton?"

No tips, no Coke seemed a legitimate grievance. The lawyer pulled five hundred dollars from his pocket.

"That should take care of it."

Deliveries resumed immediately.

During this stay Hutton ran up a bill of almost thirty thousand dollars despite her manager's concern. Management politely asked her to make at least a partial payment. The Beverly Hills didn't want to make the same mistake the Wilshire had made, allowing her tab to hit a hundred grand. She huffed a bit, paid all but sixteen hundred dollars to the Beverly Hills, and moved back to the Wilshire.

She returned for another stay at the Beverly Hills in 1976, from January 25 to February 24. On this occasion, according to a suit the hotel filed in superior court, Barbara neglected to pay for $6,950 in "goods, ware, merchandises and services."

More unseemly yet, according to the suit, Barbara had walked off with two flower pots, two dried palm plants, a two-piece bowl, and a silk flower arrangement that had been in her suite before January 25 but which weren't there a month later.

§   §   §   §   §   §   §   §   §   §

The hotel had been in superior court fourteen years earlier over a fracas with another millionaire.

This one was Samuel Genis, a real estate developer. Samuel and his wife, Sayde, had been living in the hotel since July 1949. Part of the dispute stemmed from whether the hotel had overcharged Genis in altering their suite to their specifications while the Crescent Wing was under construction. The bill came to $30,788. Genis had paid $7,500, saying the charges were excessive.

But there was more to the suit. The hotel wanted them out for more important reasons than money. They were turning the Beverly Hills into their version of a tenement. The Genises were hanging laundry on the balcony, drying sheets out the window, dumping trash in the hallways, and cursing at the help.

Not the kind of behavior welcomed at the Beverly Hills.

Chapter Twelve

Sally Kellerman, the tall, loose-limbed blonde Hot Lips Hoolihan in the movie *M*A*S*H*, flounced into David Merrick's room.

J. R., her cat, was under her arm, and Holly, her dog, was tugging on the leash.

Kellerman had hopes of landing the Holly Golightly role in Merrick's Broadway production of *Breakfast at Tiffany's*. She was too late. Mary Tyler Moore had landed it. But Merrick, dodging Holly and J. R., who were using his room as a playpen, offered Kellerman the second lead, Holly's wacky friend Mag Wildwood.

It was not what she had come for, but it was good enough. The "audition" was over and business completed, save for agents arguing salary and such.

Kellerman scooped up J. R., cornered Holly, and was on her way out, when Merrick said, "By the way, where did you rent the dog and cat, and what are their real names?"

§   §   §   §   §   §   §   §   §   §

Business as usual at the Beverly Hills is not quite business as usual elsewhere. Moguls and mogulettes in the Polo Lounge talk millions into pink phones. Tycoons and baby tycoons, soaking up rays at the pool, talk percentages cross-country to shivering New Yorkers. Companies are bought, companies are sold, fortunes rise and fall, and stars are born.

§   §   §   §   §   §   §   §   §   §

Paging Mark Goodson in the Polo Lounge. Paging Mark Goodson in the coffee shop. Paging Mark Goodson at the swimming pool.

There he sits, next to the 75-by-33½-foot pool, with two telephones and a secretary, ironing out wrinkles, coming up with ideas, discussing casting, hiring, firing, keeping his incredibly successful Goodson-Todman TV-game-show empire intact.

Goodson sometimes shows up as Svend Petersen, the handsome Danish guardian of the Pool and Cabaña Club, opens at 10:00 A.M., and he's still in the same spot working when the pool's being closed at 7:30.

Industrialist Norton Simon is another poolside worker. He likes to work where people can see him, although the pool seems an unlikely place for business.

On warm, sunny days—most of the year, in other words—oiled and browning bodies crowd around the pool, lounging on chaise longues that Svend and his pool boys solicitously turn with the movement of the sun.

From the Streetcar Named Desire, the bar cart near the entrance, waiters continually rush back and forth balancing trays of Perrier, screwdrivers, and liquored punches.

Room-service waiters appear with trays of food for the hungry at poolside and in the cabañas, which can be rented for fifteen dollars a day. The Beatles have lounged in cabañas, as has Teddy Kennedy. Leslie Caron was given an upper one, since she insisted on sunbathing topless.

Very often a cabaña is the site of a high-stakes card game. Harry Karl, Debby Reynolds's husband for a while, dropped fifty thousand dollars one unlucky afternoon.

If you don't have a cabaña, you want a lounge at the

edge of the pool. These are handed out on a first-come, first-served basis, but some people drop by to see Svend at 8 when he starts readying the area, to coax him into relaxing that rule.

Besides the bikinis and maillots preening by, tennis whites can be seen; the two tennis courts are behind the pool. Peruvian Alex Olmeda, the 1959 Australian singles champion and American indoor champion at Wimbledon, is the pro now. He charges thirty dollars an hour for his expertise.

§ § § § § § § § § §

The Polo Lounge, guarded from the glare, is a more suitable conference site. There, Paramount Pictures was sold to Charles Bludhorn's Gulf and Western.

Ann-Margret huddled with her husband, Roger Smith, and agent Alan Carr day after day trying to decide what to do with her career, which was going nowhere. The talks, day after day, laid the basis for Smith and Carr to propel her into becoming one of the highest-paid performers in Las Vegas and receiving an Academy Award nomination for *Carnal Knowledge.*

Those talks in the Polo Lounge also transformed Carr into a big-time manager—big enough so that he can now afford to be the latest Perle Mesta of Hollywood.

Not long before that trio huddled, Arthur Miller conferenced with Clark Gable in the Polo Lounge. Miller was writing his first screenplay, and he wanted Gable to play the lead.

Gable thought it ridiculous that he would appear in a work by the erudite Mr. Miller. But Miller insisted—the role was Gable.

After several hours, the king agreed to *The Misfits*, the movie that was to be his last and the last of his co-star Marilyn Monroe.

Oscar Dystal, president of Bantam Books, Inc., the nation's top paperback house, wasn't as successful as Miller.

Dystal wanted to buy a book. Hardback publisher Bernie Geis had submitted it, and Bantam had said no. Then editor Marc Jaffe changed his mind. Geis made a money demand, and Jaffe countered with a lower offer.

When the final manuscript was shown around, Jaffe expressed more interest. Geis made another money demand—much higher—and again Jaffe responded with a slightly lower offer.

Now Dystal was drinking socially with the book's author, Helen Gurley Brown, and her movie-producer husband, David, who would later become very rich as co-producer of *Jaws* and *Jaws II*. At the moment, the limelight was Helen's. (She had yet to become the fabulously successful editor of *Cosmopolitan*.)

Dystal and his wife and the Browns walked from the Polo Lounge into the lobby.

"Helen," Dystal said, "Marc likes your book, and I think we'd like to buy it."

Helen Gurley Brown smiled sweetly and kissed Oscar Dystal on the cheek. "Oscar, I love you. But you turned my book down three times, and now you couldn't have it if you were the only paperback house on earth!"

When Dystal later reported the kiss-off conversation to Bernie Geis, he added, "You owe me one!"

So Dystal didn't get *Sex and the Single Girl*, but a year or so later Geis phoned him. "Listen, I know you were disappointed about Helen's book, but I have a novel now that I think will make up for it."

And that's how the multimillion-copy *Valley of the Dolls* became a Bantam paperback.

The Beverly Hills is good stomping ground for writers and publishers.

Irwin Shaw and Cleveland Amory are part of the furniture.

Jacqueline Susann would borrow a blackboard from the kitchen, to keep track of her many characters. She would disappear for days, churning out *Once Is Not Enough, Delores,* and such.

Charming, friendly, Susann was always a favorite among the staff. Svend of the pool was even included by name in *Once Is Not Enough.*

Although Joyce Haber lived only a few blocks away, she couldn't concentrate with the household commitments around her. She took a room at the Beverly Hills while she was writing *The Users.* It is believed that Bob Evans paid for this luxury—one way to keep yourself from being painted too harshly when a you-like character is being included in a novel!

As competitive as they are, the Beverly Hills is one place publishers agree on. You're likely to find Helen Meyer or Bud Tobey of Dell in the coffee shop while Marc Jaffe of Bantam is returning service on the tennis court.

§   §   §   §   §   §   §   §   §   §

Not all business at the Beverly Hills is movies and literature.

§   §   §   §   §   §   §   §   §   §

Mr. Henry Crown was having dinner with friends in Beverly Hills.

Mr. Henry Crown is the patriarch of a family that holds great numbers of shares in such companies as General Dynamics, Hilton Hotels, Aetna Life and Casualty, St. Louis–San Francisco Railways, and many others.

In the course of dinner, the butler announced a call for Crown.

"But it can't be for me," Crown protested. "Nobody knows I'm here. Besides, the phone number here is unlisted, isn't it?"

And yet it was for him, someone "speaking for" Mr. Hughes, Howard Hughes.

Would Mr. Crown be able to talk to Mr. Hughes later tonight? Mr. Hughes will call you at your hotel.

Perplexed but curious (this was 1961, and Hughes was a mysterious figure), Crown went to his hotel to wait for the call, which didn't come until the next morning.

Despite no apologies from Hughes, the call had been worth waiting for.

TWA needed $250 million to keep from crashing into bankruptcy. And although Hughes was worth some $750 million, he needed lots of cash.

According to the *New York Times*, Hughes proposed the following deal to Crown, who wasn't caught in a cash-flow shortage: "Mr. Crown would lend Mr. Hughes $50 million, borrowed from the Bank of America using the Empire State Building as collateral. If this took place, the bank had agreed to lend another $50 million directly to Mr. Hughes. That $100 million would provide the financial underpinning that would enable Mr. Hughes to sell $150 million in securities."

It was a complex deal, but Crown had a preexisting interest in it. General Dynamics, in which he was a major stockholder, got a lot of business from TWA. In fact, TWA was its biggest civilian customer. The fate of TWA was the fate of General Dynamics.

Hughes suggested the two discuss the deal further at his Beverly Hills Hotel bungalow.

Crown took a cab to the hotel—he was spared a Sheilah Graham round-about tour—and was walking through the garden, when he heard his name whispered.

Looking around, he realized there was a tall man shadowed under a palm. It was Hughes. And there, under the palm tree, the multimillion-dollar deal was discussed. Hughes never invited Crown into his rooms, much less offered him so much as a glass of water.

Conference over, Crown's accountant started checking books, and yes, the Hughes empire was solid.

Papers were drawn up. One final detail, and the deal was closed. The detail was Howard Hughes's signature.

Officials from the Bank of America rendezvoused at the bungalow but were turned away, with no signature.

"Mr. Hughes is quite sick now," they were told by the Mormon bodyguards. "He is too weak to sign his name."

Instead he sold his TWA stock at $85 a share. He came away with $550 million on the deal.

Hughes did business in unusual spots and in bizarre ways. But he was shrewd. And shrewd meant knowing what the other fellow was doing.

The front desk received reservations for eight rooms on the ground floor for Adnan Khashoggi and his party. The group arrived in stages. A secretary, a chauffeur, and five others on the first day. His wife and her hairdresser on the second. The third day, it was Khashoggi at last, a plump man, undistinguished except for his custom-made silk suits.

Khashoggi's arrival had been preceded by a visit from a Sergeant Tracy Schnelker. What he was a sergeant of, he never made clear, but he did spell out what he wanted from the two room clerks on duty.

He wanted information. Nothing illegal and nothing that difficult. It was merely keeping track of Khashoggi's ins and outs, including his phone calls.

The clerks were to arrange it with the operator. And it was hoped that the clerks would be able to say, as Khashoggi or one of the minions passed the desk, "Gee, it's such a nice day, are you heading for the beach? Hope you're not letting business spoil the pleasure of our town?" And so forth, to extract any little hint at all about movements and whereabouts, and goings-on.

It didn't seem that difficult, and the hinted-at gratitude would make any inconvenience well worth it.

Surveillance began.

The operators were cued and ready to keep notes. The clerks were on alert.

And then, nothing. The Arabs queered the surveillance. It was never one Arab making a call. It was all of them picking up phones at the same time, from different rooms, from the lobby, from the pool, and asking for numbers. If one of Khashoggi's people made a call, the rest made calls at the exact same moment. In the flurry the operators couldn't keep track of who was calling where.

The cheerful clerks at the desk fared no better. When the Arabs went out the front, they had no comment on the weather. But usually they left by side entrances.

Sergeant Tracy Schnelker had to admit defeat, for himself and his boss, Howard Hughes.

It had been Hughes behind the operation. He had been trying to pick up a small edge in an arms deal Khashoggi was negotiating for Saudi Arabia.

Hughes, who was in the bidding with his helicopters, wanted to know with whom else Khashoggi was dealing.

For once the Beverly Hills let him down.

The switchboard operators were rewarded anyway. One clerk got $250 for his effort. The second chose to take an Ali Baba wish, "Let me know if there is anything I can ever do for you," which he has yet to collect from Sergeant Schnelker.

Chapter Thirteen

You start with a Barrymore and pretty soon it's Charlie Chaplin at this booth and Errol Flynn and Brigitte Bardot and Dean Martin and Martha Mitchell and heaven knows who else. How can you pinpoint the precise birth of a legend?

—Mal Sibley on the Polo Lounge.

It's a legend for who has been there, who's there now, and who is yet to come.

The Polo Lounge.

The most celebrated oasis for drinking and mingling in the United States.

Dark, seductive, ice cubes tingling as people flit from one round table to another, searching for the familiar and famous to greet, kiss, and gush, "Oh so lovely seeing you again." People holding court at coveted banquettes as sycophants pay their respects. People sitting goggly-eyed as it all unfolds before them.

Royalty over there. (Isn't that Princess Grace?)

Writers over here. (Allen Drury, right?)

And ohmygod, that's Steve McQueen underneath that prodigious beard! And yes, there goes Jaclyn Smith. And John Wayne . . . Rock Hudson . . . Lucille Ball . . . Faye Dunaway . . . Milton Berle . . . and no! It can't be (but it is) Cary Grant!

This is the Polo Lounge. An ogler's paradise that serves good drinks. A table-hopper's heaven where everyone who is anyone generally shows up.

Pinpoint a legend? It just grew.

Grew when John Barrymore soliloquized between sips.

When Mario Lanza burst into song.

When Ava Gardner seized a waitress and danced her into the kitchen.

And it grows each time a celebrity is interviewed over a deliciously chilled bottle of Pinot Chardonnay and Pacific bay shrimp.

"Seated at her banquette at the Polo Lounge . . ." "Nursing a Bloody Mary in the Polo Lounge . . ." "Discussing terms in the Polo Lounge . . ." Dozens of stories a year come out of that one room. It is *the* place to be seen. *The* place to be. *The* place to be welcomed and admired.

This isn't another hotel cocktail lounge. It is an institution, and it treats its patrons right.

Stars are treated like stars, and you know you're Somebody when you start getting the "good" tables in the Polo Lounge.

§   §   §   §   §   §   §   §   §   §

Carol Connors skated the fringe of fame for years. She was on her way up very young when she wrote, "To Know, Know, Know Him Is to Love, Love, Love Him." But after that, nothing much. Knocking on doors. Getting around. Trying to sell her songs, trying to be seen. All the while marking time in the Polo Lounge, but receiving that extra-special treatment only if she was with Someone Special, Someone with a Name, Someone like David Janssen.

There isn't one time in the Polo Lounge. There are four, each with its own mood, each with its own envied tables of honor. Connors would make an appearance from time to time at all of them.

Breakfast. Starting at 7:00 A.M., hostess Bernice Philbin and her ten waitresses serve Easterners trying to make the 9:00 o'clock flight to New York, talking business with Westerners they've managed to roust out of bed.

Fresh, fresh orange juice. Kadota figs. Omelets with creamed smoked salmon. Sole, steak, brioches. And of course, tea served the proper way with a second silver pot, filled with hot water.

In the morning, the favored place to dine is in the Loggia, a sun-filled fifty-seat satellite to the cocktail lounge.

(Precisely speaking, the Polo Lounge is only that dark, inside cocktail area, although most people call the Loggia and Patio that as well.)

This is the time for business. Literary agents touting manuscripts to publishers. Producers weaving storylines to backers. Executives brainstorming sales campaigns. Investors telephoning buy and sell orders to their New York brokers.

Paul Lazarus, producer of *Future World*, calls the breakfast businessing "wonderfully silly . . . curiously necessary." The agora has to be somewhere.

(Peter Finch was on his way to the Loggia for a breakfast conference with *Network* director Sidney Lumet when he collapsed in the lobby and died.)

§   §   §   §   §   §   §   §   §   §

Lunch. The beautiful and the honored move outside to the hundred-seat Patio, to be shaded by Brazilian pepper trees and surrounded by tan, blonde pulchritude, people who somehow belong in Mercedes 450-SLs.

Now it's Nino, the Latin-handsome maitre d', who bestows the best tables on silver-sunglassed Farrah Fawcett-Majors and French-jeaned Ali McGraw. Even reservations and a generous tip will not guarantee a good table from Nino. It's as much who you are as what you give that counts in the end.

The mingling and greeting begin in earnest. People who have seen each other yesterday are bussing and over-joyed to see each other again, all the while nibbling on beluga malossol caviar, Royal squab, and coconut mousse maison.

George Jessel, weighed down with his bars of medals, says hello to friends while lunching with two teenaged girls at his side.

Writers John Gregory Dunne and Joan Didion partake of the scene and the food with daughter Quitanna Roo, while sun sparkles off Julie Andrews.

§   §   §   §   §   §   §   §   §   §

The afternoon stretches into cocktail time, Polo Lounge time, 5:00 to 7:30 P.M.

Ostensibly there are 120 seats in the lounge, clustered around intimate round tables, perfectly shaped for tête-à-têtes. The special places, however, the desirable spots for your Margaritas, are the banquettes that face the door, the vantage spots to see everyone coming and going and carrying on.

The room curves around from this front section, and although the tables in the back are only A minus, they are still in the Polo Lounge. Siberia is now the Patio, where you don't have a chance at the enormous platters of crackers, Cheddar cheese, tortilla chips, and luscious, drooled-over guacamole.

Polo Lounge guacamole.

It's a test of character to hold out, to see if your table will be blessed with a free plate of the goodies—they appear at six and not before. If you succumb and have to have the dip at five minutes to six, it costs fifteen dollars.

Tables on the Patio never get the free avacado delight.

Buzz-buzz. Hug-hug. The pace of mingling and greeting picks up.

Jack Nicholson here. Warren Beatty there. Carol Burnett in the corner. The tourists that manage to get in, after a wait, have trouble assimilating it all.

It may be silly, pretentious, but it is fun.

Especially if you are Carol Connors and you've been on the fringe and now you're an "overnight" hot property for writing thirty little words, the words to the theme song of *Rocky*.

Bam, bam.

Connors is nominated for an Academy Award.

Bam, bam.

She is scoring for Disney.

Bam, bam.

Her dates are getting mentioned in the *Hollywood Reporter*.

"Applauding Buddy Greco's smash bow at the London Club: Henry Berger and Carol Connors."

"New Two for Bananas Laureate at the Coterie: Carol Connors and Harvey Chaplin."

"Party popped at Julie and Herb Hutner's BevHills manse with about 100 celebs quaffing their favorite brew, including . . . Carol Connors adding Bob Sakowitz to her long dating string."

All wonderful and exhilarating, but it wasn't until Walter, the maitre d' in the evening, started giving her choice tables that she knew she had made it.

"I was always treated well there," Connors said. "But then one night Walter started talking enthusiastically to me about how he never knew what I did. Never knew I was a songwriter. 'I don't like to talk about myself,' I explained. 'That in itself is extraordinary,' Walter said."

§   §   §   §   §   §   §   §   §   §

Legends.

Marlene Dietrich behind one of the banquette tables,

elegantly complaining to *the* press agent of that time, Russell (the Bird) Birdwell, that it had become quite tedious being known as the woman with the world's best legs.

"Wear pants," Birdwell suggested.

She did and earned a niche in fashion history by introducing pantsuits to the women of the world.

Legends.

Mia Farrow being turned away from the Polo Lounge because she was wearing a pantsuit. Brigitte Bardot not getting in because she was barefoot. Anita Ekberg made to wear that silly pink coverup.

The Polo Lounge has an image, and it maintains it. For years a woman in slacks was not permitted. If she insisted on staying, the maitre d' provided her with a pink wraparound skirt that looked suspiciously like a tablecloth.

Even today, men must wear jackets after 7:00 P.M.

One, *Los Angeles Herald Examiner* columnist Denis Hamill (Pete's brother), had the distinction of being tossed out when he came sans coat and refused to pay the cigarette girl for the use of an extra one she happened to have.

Legends.

Yes, there is a cigarette girl at the Polo Lounge, complete with cigarette tray strapped around her neck, as if she were answering a casting call for a George Raft nightclub scene.

Buddy the page would certainly land a role in the same movie. Four feet tall, in his brass-buttoned jacket and red-striped pants, he periodically marches through the lounge yelling 'Ca-ll fo-ooh Miz Men-gas!" "Ca-ll fo-ooh Mist-ah La-zar." When someone picks up his or her hand in acknowledgment, Buddy produces a pink phone to be plugged in at the table. And isn't it fun to be able to say, "Yes, could you speak up a little? I'm in the Polo Lounge and Cassavettes and Peter Falk are cutting up at the next table"?

Some Polo Lounge denizens may have seen too many

movies. Usually single fellows, they sit with the phones plastered to their ears as if imitating some glamorized notion of Irving Thalberg.

But Buddy makes his rounds and reaps his profits. "Ca-ll fo-oh Ro-bert Mit-chum." "Ca-ll for Ar-nold Pahl-mer."

There is the story that one night some of the New York Knicks, making the scene after a game with the Lakers, stretched their legs out in the Polo Lounge.

One spotted Buddy.

"And what position do you play?" he asked.

"I'm the bouncer," Buddy answered. "And if you don't behave yourself I'll get on a chair and kick you in the shins."

With the considerable tips he's made—he's been at the Beverly Hills for more than twenty years—Buddy is reported to have extensive real estate holdings.

Buddy gives you your messages, but it is Harris, the waiter, who "knows where the action is."

Although the hotel management would like to believe it isn't true—hookers don't enhance a chic image—prostitutes do work the Polo Lounge. Discreetly. It's a matter of knowing whom to ask.

Dino Borelli, a former cocktail-hour maitre d', said a few years ago, "We watch for the professional women. I can spot them. You see two women coming in alone dressed in a certain way—their eyes searching the room for game—and you know they're pros.

"I meet them at the door and say that we do not allow unescorted women after 8. Or after 9. Or after 10.

"Of course, you miss sometimes and try to keep out legitimate customers, and they raise hell and demand to see the manager. Then, of course, we realize their legitimacy and allow them in."

He added that he would sometimes pair up unescorted women with gentlemen by seating them nearby. "If they get together, then fun is fun. No one is an angel. The men can go back to Schenectady and say, 'Boy, the stuff on the loose at the Polo Lounge!' It adds to the legend. But we are in reality the cleanest place in town."

Perhaps, but the girls are there and working. Some are only semi-pro, hoping for little more than a good meal and a small gift. Others work for the madame who drives up twice a week in the purple limo to check out her stable.

The madame's girls charge one hundred dollars for fifteen minutes, two thousand dollars for an entire night. (They complain about the English rock stars who've been staying at the hotel lately. British rock stars don't bathe enough, the girls say.)

Then there are the girls who have been known to cruise the hallways in the main building, knocking on doors until they find a receptive gentleman.

Management attempted to cut down on libidinous action in the Polo Lounge by not admitting unescorted women and by not allowing women to perch at the bar, near the front wall. This earned the hotel a spot on the women's-liberation hit list.

Three women, accompanied by television cameras, tried to get served at the bar and were, they claimed, "bodily thrown out." The American Civil Liberties Union sued for $180,500 in damages.

A spokesperson for the ACLU said the bar's policy "reflects the archaic notion that so-called nice women do not sit at the bar alone or with other women.

"The fact that the Polo Lounge is willing to seat women at a table does not mitigate the effect of being refused service at the bar."

Hookers usually work the Polo Lounge during its fourth period, the time after the cocktail hour when the crowd has finished off the piquant and delightful guacamole, downed their drinks, and drifted off to La Scala, Le Bistro or some other swank restaurant.

The Polo Lounge is quiet, anticipating the night people who drift in and out until closing at 2:00 A.M. This is the time that Russell Birdwell was referring to when he called the Polo Lounge "a place, strangely enough, for lonely people. I mean, who in the hell in Beverly Hills doesn't have his own bar at home? So they don't go to the Polo Lounge to just drink. They go there to visit or to have visitors as if it's their own home."

The Polo Lounge at night is the haven for chain-bedecked swingers trying to score points with their dates.

"Walter, how are you, Walter? Harris, it's been a long time. Well, I've been working hard. Yeah, I'm driving a Vega because my Porsche is in the shop." This last remark, naturally, was the same one he gave the car jockeys at the entrance.

There can be steam and movement at night also. More than enough the night Frank Sinatra begged to differ with the opinion of a visiting businessman. Ol' Blue Eyes slugged him. Dean Martin came to the aid of his crooning buddy by jumping into the fracas. Both he and Sinatra were ejected and told that their presence at the Beverly Hills was no longer appreciated.

There was the night that Dino, the maitre d', noticed Jackie Gleason had fallen asleep at his table. Gleason, with a reputation for boozing, was attracting a lot of stares. Dino, with the grace of a true diplomat, stood by Gleason for twenty minutes, carrying on an animated conversation with the zonked comedian—all one-sided, of course.

Finally Gleason opened an eye.

"Dino," he said, "you're full of it."

§   §   §   §   §   §   §   §   §   §

Just as in the hotel, guests are shielded and guarded in the Polo Lounge. It is supposed to be a place where celebrities can meet and not be bothered by autograph-seeking hordes. Although there was one long-time waiter who Boswelled the place with his autograph books. They were the only ones allowed, and he had all the signatures from when the Polo Lounge first opened, although he said he treasured the "To my good friend, Willie, Salvador Dali" the most.

The waiters are usually not allowed to insinuate themselves on the guest. It keeps hopeful actors from making a Polo Lounge waiter's job a way to producers.

On one occasion, an actor was working as a waiter. Tony Faramus. He found himself waiting on Bryan Forbes, a director he had worked with several times in London. But the hotel policy stopped him from saying, "Hi. Remember me?"

As luck would have it, Forbes knew he knew Tony's face from somewhere and broached the subject himself. The upshot was Faramus got a role in Forbes's next movie, *King Rat*.

To cut down on celebrity gawking and ogling, there is no mirror behind the bar. Instead it's a mural of Persian polo players.

If there wasn't this attention to privacy, how would Cary Grant have been able to counsel Lance Reventlow on the ins and outs and safest maneuvers in obtaining a divorce from Jill St. John? Grant was experienced in the matter, having been married to and unmarried from Lance's own mother, Barbara Hutton, among others. (St. John had been promised a million in jewels by Mama Hutton if she could get Lance to give up auto racing. She didn't and never got the gift. On the other hand, Lance's widow, former Mouseketeer Cheryl, is supported by Hutton, who hopes eventually to get his ashes.)

§   §   §   §   §   §   §   §   §   §

According to the all-knowing *New York* magazine, there is a group that is taking over Hollywood.

Baby moguls they've been dubbed, war-demonstration survivors who have new values and are bringing a new order to the movie industry.

These newcomers sneer at the "Polio" Lounge and at the Bob Evans mentality of big mansions with screening rooms.

Give them five years, ten for the diehards, and they, too, will be glued to their little chairs in the Polo Lounge, chattering, sipping their Perrier, dipping into the status-filled guacamole with studied indifference.

As the first hint of sunlight caresses in from the east, the Mexican gardeners begin their watering and pruning.

In the kitchen a chef yawns, hopes for a slow day, and then studies the list of things to be done.

A hall porter finishes vacuuming the main lobby while an early-morning arrival is dispassionately told that her room won't be ready before noon.

Slumber is over. The jasmine mixes with hyacinth and oleander. The hotel begins to come to life in a hundred ways, all at once.

Someone unlocks the door to the Polo Lounge. An operator rings through Mr. Slatkin's wake-up call.

In front a carhop places the car-key envelopes in the wall file.

In bungalow 7, an Eastern guest who has been dancing late at Daisy squints at the golden-brilliant California sun before deciding to doze off again.

No more mist. No more night.

Phones are ringing as the full complement of switchboard operators adjust their headsets and settle in for another rushed day. Room service swings into its efficient pace. A breakfast tray is pushed along the path, jingling as it rounds curves, giving off delectable aromas.

The Beverly Hills Hotel is in action. And indeed, today, like every day, the Pink Palace is where the action will be.

INDEX